Tales from the
COLORADO ROCKIES

Tony DeMarco

SportsPublishingLLC.com

ISBN 13: 978-1-59670-2325

Publishers: Peter L. Bannon and Joseph J. Bannon Sr.
Senior managing editor: Susan M. Moyer
Art director: Dustin J. Hubbart

Sports Publishing L.L.C.
804 North Neil Street
Champaign, IL 61820
Phone: 1-877-424-2665
Fax: 1-217-363-2073
www.SportsPublishingLLC.com

Printed in the United States of America

CIP data available upon request

To Alexandra, my one and only

CONTENTS

FOREWORD

There has never been a better time to be a Rockies fan. We are coming off our first pennant, and the amazing 21-of-22 streak that got us there, and head into the 2008 season anticipating more great things to come.

What you watched unfold at the end of last season was the culmination of a long building process, the result of an entire organization working together toward a common goal: putting a team on the field that our fans can be proud of.

It was a long time in coming, and required patience along the way, but I believe we are prepared for the future through our past. In this book, you will read about our franchise's history from a trusted reporter who has been around our team as long as I have. And as someone who has been in the organization since 1994, I am proud to say the future of the Colorado Rockies looks bright.

—Rockies manager Clint Hurdle, February 2008

THE STREAK THAT CHANGED A FRANCHISE

OVER THE HUMP

Dan O'Dowd sat in his Coors Field office two weeks before the first 2007 spring training workout, and spoke from his heart. His words rang true with conviction; but even in his most optimistic moment, he probably didn't believe that what he was saying would burst to full fruition just eight months later in such an unexpected, amazing, and record-setting fashion that the Colorado Rockies franchise—downtrodden for nearly a full decade after a memorable beginning—took on a new aura and identity. That's what happens when you win 21 of 22 games on your way to a National League pennant.

"It may take more time for some of these kids," O'Dowd said that morning. "But the talent level we have throughout our organization is better than at any time in our history. We've never had this kind of depth. Now it's a matter of getting over the hump. We got over the hump when I was in Cleveland. We had a very long winning streak at home in 1995, and our confidence and belief went to a different level.

"I had a conversation last winter with (former Twins general manager) Terry Ryan, and I asked him: was there a point when you knew? He said no, but one year they had a young club, they thought they could be good, and they went something like 18-6 in April. From there on out, it totally changed their organization. The confidence, the belief, the swagger—it all comes with knowing you can win.

"That hasn't happened here yet. But it's going to happen. When it happens we'll be a completely different club. We will be a dominant club. We will be a team people don't want to play."

Well, it's happened, all right, and it's been a magical ride for the Rockies, from Todd Helton's walkoff home run that beat the Los Angeles Dodgers on September 17 to a dominating sweep of the Arizona Diamondbacks in the National League Championship Series that put them over the hump and on top of the National League.

Not even a disappointing World Series sweep at the hands of the powerful Boston Red Sox has done much damage to the Rockies' newfound standing. They are the latest model of modest-payroll, build-from-within success, and you can bet other organizations around the game are saying, "If the Rockies can do it, why not us?"

The Rockies as a model organization? You bet, and here's how their run unfolded in all its head shaking, is-this-really-happening? glory.

MORE THAN A FEELING

O'Dowd wasn't the only one in the organization who had an inkling of what was to come late in 2007. Vinny Castilla, one of the original Blake Street Bombers, also saw better things on the way.

"I've never seen so many young kids be so good at the same time," Castilla said late in 2006. "We had a lot of talent in 1995, but we weren't that young. These kids are young, and they're good. I think this is going to be a very good team for the next couple of years."

Walt Weiss, another remnant of the club's early glory years, and like Castilla, now a special assistant to O'Dowd, echoed his former teammate's thoughts:

"Doing what I'm doing, I see the big picture," Weiss said at the end of the 2006 season. "I get out and see the minor leaguers. I see the big leaguers when I'm here. I've got a pretty good perspective of what they're trying to do as an organization. The fans don't see it all quite yet, but it's about to happen. I truly believe that."

But winning a National League pennant in 2007? Nobody expected that, and the season sure didn't begin with that expectation in mind.

Opening Day at Coors Field last season wasn't exactly a festive one. The Rockies slapped around Diamondbacks ace Brandon Webb, only to see their bullpen give up three runs in the eighth inning of an 8-6 loss.

But the real head shaking occurred around the stadium and especially in the press box, with the announcement that O'Dowd and manager Clint Hurdle had been given two-year contract extensions.

O'Dowd, on the job since late in 1999, had produced only one winning year, and barely at that at 82-80 in 2000. Since Hurdle had been promoted from hitting instructor to manager in late April of 2002, the Rockies' biggest season win total was 76 in 2006. And yet these two received two-year extensions to keep them out of potential lame-duck situations?

At one point during his tenure, when criticism was at a high, Hurdle had said, "Sure it's fair. I don't think there are many jobs in society that you can be mediocre in and keep."

And looking back a few days before winning the NLCS, Hurdle admitted: "I was caught off guard (by the extension). When it was offered, it didn't take me long to agree to take it. I'm not that good in math, but I thought two more years was a pretty good idea."

All the justification needed for those extensions, however, unfolded in one of the most compelling and dramatic late-season runs in baseball history. It's when a nice building-block of a season—the Rockies were 76-72 when their run began—spiked sharply upward and became something entirely different, even franchise-changing. So in the midst of the wildcard-clinching celebration in the home clubhouse at Coors Field on October 1, owner Charlie Monfort was asked about the justification.

"Yes, there is some, but that's not the reason why we did it," Monfort said. "We wanted to take the focus off Dan and Clint. We have a young team. We didn't want them worrying about whether Dan and Clint would be here tomorrow if we weren't playing well. We believe our organization is as strong as it can be, and Clint has made great strides. We have stability here."

Yes, the Rockies became a national story with their historic 21-1 run to the pennant, but the fact is, they had the best record in the league from late May and the league's best ERA after the All-Star break. And the framework from which the run emerged had been in place for the last couple seasons. A rebuilding process began in 2004, and by 2005, core players Matt Holliday, Jeff Francis, Garrett Atkins, Brad Hawpe, and Brian Fuentes were establishing themselves at the major-league level.

There were also smart bargain-basement pickups of key contributors Kazuo Matsui, Yorvit Torrealba, and Matt Herges, along with the important acquisitions of Willy Taveras, Taylor Buchholz, and Jason Hirsh for Jason Jennings.

A decision not to deal Todd Helton to the Red Sox in the winter of 2006-07 kept the team's franchise player in place, even at the cost of his $16.6-million annual salary that put a strain on the payroll.

There was the inspiring and stunningly mature play of rookie shortstop Troy Tulowitzki, the poster boy for a farm system ranked at the top of the game. Almost as important was the emergence of ice-cool Manuel Corpas in the closer role after Fuentes faltered.

And when things looked bleak in early August—when three starting pitchers went on the disabled list in a two-week span—up from the minors came the overpowering arms of Ubaldo Jimenez and Franklin Morales, the two best physical talents ever to step on a mound in Rockies history.

Still, after two consecutive losses at Coors Field to the last-place Florida Marlins, the Rockies stood 4½ games behind in the wildcard race on September 15, with three teams to pass. It didn't take a sabermetrician to figure out the Rockies were up against a challenge. Only 14 games remained, and a miracle was needed.

And that's exactly what occurred.

THIRTEEN OF FOURTEEN

The Los Angeles Dodgers arrived at Coors Field for a four-game series beginning September 17, having no idea that their season was

Jeff Francis won 17 games and developed into the staff ace in 2007. *AP Images*

about to disintegrate. The spiral of clubhouse troubles and on-field collapse that led to Grady Little's resignation and Joe Torre's hiring began with a 3-1 loss in Game 1 of a doubleheader.

Then came the blow that sent two teams' seasons in diametrically opposite directions: bottom of the ninth in the nightcap, Dodgers leading 8-7, and Rockies nemesis Takashi Saito, in the midst of a brilliant season, was on the mound. How good had Saito been against the Rockies up to that point? In six games, he had earned five saves without allowing a single hit.

Saito got two quick outs and it appeared as if he would notch another clean save, but then Holliday singled. Helton later belted a hanging slider 418 feet into the seats in right-center field for the game-winner, celebrating with a sprint around the bases and a flying leap into a rowdy mosh pit of teammates.

"I don't know when I'll come off that high," Helton said afterward. It turned out he wouldn't until the World Series.

The Rockies gained only half a game that night, and were still 4½ back with 11 games remaining. But Helton's rare show of elation seemed to stoke teammates who looked to him as their leader. In fact, when asked during the NLCS for one moment that sparked the Rockies' run, Francis quickly answered: "The first one that comes to mind is when Helton hit that walk-off home run off the Dodgers."

The Dodgers fell the next two nights as well, and the Rockies were on their way to San Diego where they would face the wildcard leaders. The first game was the key to the series, as they ran up against Cy Young Award winner Jake Peavy, but Morales matched Peavy pitch for pitch, and Hawpe gave the Rockies a 1-0 lead in the seventh with an RBI single. Corpas' rare slipup—a game-tying, ninth-inning homer by Adrian Gonzalez—sent the game into extra innings, and it was Hawpe who untied it with a home run off left-hander Joe Thatcher in the 14th. Herges pitched a second scoreless inning to save it, and the Rockies went on to sweep the series with 6-2 and 7-3 victories, the latter being Francis' 17th win—the most in franchise history by a left-hander.

With six games remaining, the deficit was now 1½ games, with the Padres and Philadelphia Phillies standing in the way, and who better than the reeling, in-fighting Dodgers to be next on the schedule? Historically, Dodger Stadium hasn't been a friendly place for the Rockies, but this time history could be tossed aside.

Tulowitzki's sixth-inning home run put the Rockies in the lead to stay, and they won the opener 9-7. Then Josh Fogg and three relievers combined for an eight-hit shutout, and Matsui and Holliday had RBI hits in the third inning that held up for a 2-0 win in Game 2. The series finale was a 10-4 blowout in which Morales tied the club record at 20 consecutive scoreless innings, and Helton, Atkins, and Hawpe belted home runs.

That left three games with the Diamondbacks at Coors Field to close the season—the Rockies' only hiccup in almost a month. Webb was effective in the series opener, but Francis wasn't at his best, allowing four runs in seven innings, and the Diamondbacks clinched a playoff spot with a 4-2 victory that snapped the Rockies' winning streak at 11 games.

Didn't matter. They would start another one that would last 10 games and take them to the World Series, though not without a little help from their friends, specifically, Tony Gwynn Jr. of the Milwaukee Brewers.

About four hours from game time on Saturday afternoon, there were so many reporters in the Rockies' clubhouse to watch the all-important Padres-Brewers finish in Milwaukee that one player shouted, "What, is the press box closed?"

In truth, reporters were lingering in case the Rockies were eliminated from playoff contention with a Padres victory. At a tense moment late in that game, Hawpe grabbed the remote, flipped to a college football game, and said, "Is this all right?" It told you something about how the Rockies were able to accomplish what they did; besides playing remarkably well, they played loose, with no outside expectations, no pressure.

But to keep their chances alive, they needed Gwynn to line a triple into the right-field corner off legendary closer Trevor Hoffman to send the game into extra innings, allowing unknown rookie Vinny Rottino to win it with a single in the bottom of the 11th.

Of course, they also needed the Brewers to win on the final day of the regular season, and themselves to beat the Diamondbacks on the final two days. They achieved this—11-1 and 4-3—with a three-run rally in the bottom of the eighth of the latter game, when Hawpe's two-out, two-run RBI double proved to be the game-winning hit.

Concurrently, the New York Mets were imploding in historic fashion. Somehow, they frittered away a lead that was as big as seven games on September 12, and came up both one game short of the Phillies in the National League East and one game short of the Padres and Rockies in the wildcard race. Tied at 89-73, the Rockies and Padres had an October 1 date at Coors Field to determine the wildcard winner.

"We had to win 13 of 14 just to get to a play-in game. That might scare you just to think about it," Francis said. "It's pretty special that it happened."

INSTANT CLASSIC

A couple of hours before the wildcard tie-breaker game, Padres manager Bud Black sat in the visitors dugout at Coors Field and tried his best before a media gathering to put a confident spin on his team's chances. After all, the Padres saved Peavy for the occasion, while the Rockies had to throw Fogg, the No. 5 starter who picked up the nickname "Dragon Slayer" after beating a handful of top-flight starters during the regular season.

But that's about the only thing on paper that favored the Padres, and no matter what anybody in a blue-and-sandstone road uniform said, there was an underlying feeling of doom on that side of the field. The Padres had blown not one but two chances to clinch the wildcard spot, losing twice in Milwaukee to close the regular season, and had to jump on a charter, fly to Denver, and face the hottest team in baseball— a team that had outscored opponents 93-43 in winning 13 of 14, on their home turf in a one-game showdown.

That said, it took the Rockies until the bottom of the 13th to pull out a victory, an instant classic of a game complete with 17 runs and 29 hits, a couple of lead changes, and a controversial finish after four hours and 40 minutes of incredible baseball.

"You may live the rest of your life and not see a better baseball game," bench coach Jamie Quirk told *The Denver Post* afterward.

The Rockies built an early 3-0 lead against a not-quite-right Peavy, but Fogg was blasted for five runs in the top of the third, including Gonzalez's huge grand slam. Single runs in the third, fifth, and sixth innings gave the Rockies a one-run lead, but Fuentes couldn't hold it in the eighth, and after that nobody could score through four innings of bullpen dominance.

A two-run homer by Scott Hairston set it up for Hoffman, the game's

Matt Holliday crossed home plate head-first with the winning run in the wildcard-clinching game against the Padres. *AP Images*

all-time save leader (though never as effective in Coors Field as elsewhere), and sure enough, the Rockies lit him up. Matsui and Tulowitzki hit back-to-back doubles for the first run, Holliday tripled to deep right field to tie it, and then Jamey Carroll lifted a liner to right field.

With no outs, you wouldn't have blamed Holliday if he stayed put on the shallow drive in Brian Giles' direction. But Holliday never hesitated, barreled into catcher Michael Barrett, his left hand getting spiked by the Padre catcher's left foot, and never touched the plate. But umpire Tim McClelland ruled him safe, setting off a raucous celebration that stretched from the field to the clubhouse.

His chin scraped red from a head-first slide, his hand bruised from the collision, Holliday said, "The umpire called me safe. That's all I know. I don't know what happened, to tell you the truth."

What had happened was more of the Rockies' magic, and it wasn't about to run out just yet.

SWEEP NO. 1

A funny feeling swept over the Rockies as they prepared to meet the Phillies in the division series: they realized that they could afford to lose a game and not be eliminated in the best-of-five series, a luxury they hadn't enjoyed over the last two weeks.

Not that they were going to lose any games, of course. Not even at Citizens Bank Park, the bandbox home of the Phillies and their rambunctious fans who have been known to intimidate opposing teams on occasion. The Rockies had just been there in mid-September, when they split a four-game series, and now they were the hottest team entering the postseason in the last three decades.

Francis went 3-0 on lead-off hitter Jimmy Rollins in the bottom of the first, but came back to strike him out, as well as the next three hitters—Shane Victorino, Chase Utley, and Ryan Howard. That set the tone for the entire game, as the Phils' top four hitters went 0-for-12 with nine strikeouts, including four by Utley and three by Howard.

The Rockies scored three runs in the second off Cole Hamels on three hits and three walks, while scoreless innings from LaTroy Hawkins, Fuentes, and Corpas protected a 4-2 Game 1 victory.

Morales allowed a home run to Rollins on the first pitch in the bottom of the first inning of Game 2 and looked skittish in his three innings, but Fogg settled things down with two scoreless innings in relief, and Matsui provided more than enough offense with two big swings of his bat. The first was a fourth-inning grand slam off Kyle Lohse that gave the Rockies a 6-3 lead. The second was an insurance-RBI triple in the midst of a four-run sixth inning of what turned into an easy 10-5 victory.

With a 2-0 lead and the series heading back to Coors Field, where they had won 39 of their last 54 games, the Rockies were in control. And they didn't let things drag out. The Game 3 pitching matchup was one of extreme opposites—23-year-old right-handed flame-throwing Jimenez against 44-year-old left-hander Jamie Moyer and his three speeds of deliveries: slow, slower, and slowest. They dueled brilliantly, with Victorino's homer tying it 1-1 in the top of the seventh.

With two outs and nobody on in the bottom of the eighth, Atkins, Hawpe, and pinch-hitter Jeff Baker all singled off reliever J.C. Romero, the latter while closer Brett Myers warmed up in the bullpen. Corpas pitched a scoreless top of the ninth to save it, and a 2-1 Game 3 victory gave the Rockies their first-ever playoff series victory.

The only thing that slowed them down—albeit temporarily—was a 14-minute delay due to light failure in the top of the second inning. But the lights weren't going out yet on the Rockies. They had one more step to take to prove what had already become obvious at this point— they were the best team in the National League.

SWEEP NO. 2

By the time the NLCS rolled around, the Diamondbacks had to be regretting not taking out the Rockies when they had the chance. After manager Bob Melvin's overachieving young team clinched a playoff spot on the last Friday of the regular season, they celebrated late into the night at Coors Field, and then didn't run their best lineup out the following two days, when one more Rockies loss would have put San Diego in the playoffs.

Yes, the Diamondbacks swept the punchless Chicago Cubs in their division series, but couldn't have wanted any part of a Rockies machine that at this point had won 17 of 18, and doubled up on opponents in terms of runs scored in that span.

Yet for all their offense, this was a Rockies team that won with pitching and defense; in fact, the latter established a major-league record for fielding percentage. And a long-held Hurdle belief—

"offensive numbers get you to the All-Star Game, but if you can pitch and field, you're going to win championships"—was playing out true to form.

In some respects, these two teams were mirror images. Both with relatively young rosters, both built mostly from within, with spring-training facilities a couple of miles apart in Tucson, and a few executives and players having history in both places.

On the eve of Game 1, ex-Rockies pitcher and scout Jerry Dipoto—now a part of the Diamondbacks' front office—captured the spirit of the rivalry by saying, "it's nice, all warm and fuzzy that the Rockies are in the playoffs. But I still want to kick their butts." The Rockies were about to prove who ruled the National League.

Any semblance of nicety disappeared in a 5-1 Game 1 victory that turned heated and ugly with Justin Upton's hard seventh-inning slide into Matsui. Upton was called out for interference on the play, cutting short a potential Diamondbacks rally, and fans disliked the call so much that they showered the field with debris, temporarily halting the game.

The Rockies had built a four-run lead at that point, knocking around Webb—the only pitcher who had beaten them since September 15—for four runs in the first three innings. The key three-run top of the third consisted of four singles, a walk, a stolen base, and a wild pitch, but that was more than enough for Francis and four relievers.

Once Webb was beaten on his home mound, everything else just fell into place for the Rockies. Take Game 2's hero, for instance. Taveras was activated for the NLCS after missing 24 games with a strained quadriceps, and he was the pivotal player in three key moments of a 3-2, 11-inning win that didn't end until 11:45 p.m. Pacific Time, thanks to TBS's insistence on a late starting time in Phoenix.

Taveras' speed helped manufacture a tie-breaking run in the fifth after he led off with a single. He made an acrobatic, diving catch in deep right-center field in the seventh inning, robbing Tony Clark of a game-tying extra-base hit, and then he worked a gassed Jose Valverde for a bases-loaded walk that scored the winning run in the top of the 11th.

With two wins on the road, did anybody think the Rockies wouldn't win the series at that point? It took only two more games at Coors Field—two sold-out, glorious-moment memories that will stick with Rockies fans for a generation or two. Not that there was any Chamber of Commerce weather for Game 3, played in very cold and rainy conditions that held down scoring.

Fogg and Livan Hernandez were in the midst of a 1-1 tie in the sixth when one swing of Torrealba's bat decided things. Former battery mates in San Francisco, Hernandez and Torrealba dueled through a seven-pitch at-bat before Hernandez caught too much of the inside part of the plate with a fastball, and Torrealba smashed it through the mist and into the left-field seats.

Three more scoreless bullpen innings from Jeremy Affeldt, Fuentes, and Corpas locked it up, and the Rockies needed only one more win for the National League pennant. One more win on top of a streak that had reached 20 wins in 21 games.

"It's crazy if you think about it," Torrealba said afterward. "It really is. That's why we don't think about it. We are just enjoying the ride."

Nobody had ever compared the 2007 Rockies to the 1976 Cincinnati Reds, but now was the time. Only those "Big Red Machine" Reds, dotted with future Hall of Famers, had swept the first two rounds in the playoffs—in their case, the NLCS and World Series. But now they had company—the Rockies.

With a 6-4 victory in Game 4—all six runs coming in a bottom of the fourth that featured a two-run double by Seth Smith and a three-run homer by Holliday—the Rockies completed the sweep. Only Fuentes' struggles in a three-run eighth marred a superbly pitched game capped by Corpas' four-out save, and the Rockies held the Diamondbacks to only eight runs in the series.

"World Class!" is what the headline atop *The Denver Post* screamed, and the jubilation on Hurdle's face captured the moment perfectly. So unexpected, such a long time coming—this was a truth-is-stranger-than-fiction moment to be cherished.

"It's a dream come true, and I'll never forget it," Atkins said.

EIGHT DAYS A WEEK

Over the course of a month, the Rockies lost only one game in 22 tries. Then over a two-week period, they couldn't win a single one. Eight days off between the NLCS sweep and Game 1 of the World Series, then four consecutive losses to the Red Sox, and the Rockies' remarkable run ended with a distinct thud.

There's no way of knowing, of course, just what might have happened if the Rockies hadn't needed to wait so long after dismissing the Diamondbacks. With only a couple days off, perhaps they would have made a much better showing, won at least a game or two, and maybe even pulled off the monumental upset.

But eight days off sapped the amazing momentum built from their run, left them out of sync and looking a bit overwhelmed in the face of the Red Sox—a team that played nearly flawless baseball in all phases, belying their reputation of being just a bunch of sluggers. Added to that was Josh Beckett, the hottest postseason pitcher on the planet. Going against him after eight days off and their timing gone gave Rockies hitters little chance in Game 1. When the Red Sox pounded Francis and put 13 runs on the board by the bottom of the fifth, a World Series appearance that was 15 years in the making turned terribly ugly.

The Rockies managed only a lone run and six hits off Beckett, while the Sox unleashed a 17-hit attack started by Dustin Pedroia's leadoff homer in the bottom of the first, and they were aided by eight walks and a ball. In a disastrous fifth, Morales was charged with seven runs in two-thirds of an inning, and Ryan Speier issued three consecutive bases-loaded walks.

"A beating," is what Helton called it, and the Rockies would never

---

Todd Helton and Troy Tulowitzki celebrate following the pennant-clinching victory.
AP Images

fully recover.

But they did have their chances to win all three remaining games, losing twice by one run and in the other game trailing by one into the eighth inning.

Jimenez vs. Curt Schilling was the Game 2 pitching matchup, and the veteran had nothing on the phenom, as the game was tied at one into the bottom of the fifth. But that's when Mike Lowell's double into the corner gave the Sox a 2-1 lead, and that's exactly how it ended, as Hideki Okajima retired seven consecutive Rockies hitters and Jonathan Papelbon got the final four outs.

But it was the first of those final four outs, the one that ended the top of the eighth, that was an absolute dagger to the Rockies' hopes. Holliday singled, and, knowing that Papelbon rarely attempted pickoffs and needing to get into scoring position, he took a huge lead. But then Papelbon crossed him up, made the pickoff throw, and caught Holliday embarrassingly far off first base.

"I wanted to cry," Holliday said afterward. Then he shook his head. "No, it's part of the game." Part of a 2-1 loss that put the Rockies in a 0-2 hole.

Coors Field had been many things in its 13-year history—home of a 200-plus-game consecutive sellout streak, site of the 1998 All-Star Game, and venue for almost-nightly offensive freak shows before anybody ever thought to store game balls in a humidor. But until Game 3, never before had it been the center of the baseball universe.

The Red Sox spoiled this mile-high celebration, however, with a six-run third inning, with most of the damage coming against Fogg, who allowed nine of 10 consecutive hitters to reach base, including seven on hits.

The Rockies rallied twice, scoring two runs in the fifth, when Ryan Spilborghs sent a blast to the center-field wall and just missed a three-run homer that would have cut the deficit to one. Holliday did

Ubaldo Jimenez could have stardom in his future.
AP Images

eventually make it a one-run game with a three-run bomb to deep center in the seventh, but another Fuentes blowup—this one for three runs—put away a 10-6 Red Sox win.

That left the finale, and its ironic pitching matchup: Aaron Cook vs. Jon Lester. Cook hadn't been on a big-league mound in more than two months after suffering an oblique injury. But that was the least of his comebacks, as he recovered from a life-threatening blood-clotting problem in 2004 that took two surgeries to correct. Lester, meanwhile, had survived a bout with cancer.

As well as Cook pitched—three runs in six-plus innings, the last coming on a home run by series MVP Lowell—Lester was better. The left-hander allowed only three hits and three walks in 5.2 shutout innings.

Torrealba hit a solo homer in the seventh, but Fuentes served one up to Bobby Kielty in the top of the eighth, which proved to be the margin of victory, as Atkins hit a two-run shot in the bottom of the eighth to make it 4-3. Enter Papelbon, and four batters (and four outs) later, the Red Sox were celebrating their second World Series title in four years.

There was disappointment in the Rockies' clubhouse afterward, but not without pride and a sense of accomplishment as well. After all, nobody could take away what the Rockies did to get there—21 wins in 22 games—even if they didn't win one in the World Series.

Monfort addressed his team privately, and then saluted them before a couple of media members. He spoke of the near future, when the goal would be to win the World Series, not just get there, and of keeping the core of the roster together, with the help of fan support that evoked memories of the way things used to be in the early years of the franchise.

The historic late September/October run is undoubtedly the latest and best chapter in the Rockies' 15-year history, but so much more had been packed into the years leading up to it.

2

A ROCKY BEGINNING

THE FRANCHISE THAT ALMOST WASN'T

Jerry McMorris was heading home from his Nations Way trucking company office one Saturday morning in August of 1992 when his cell phone rang.

It was Paul Jacobs, the Rockies' general counsel and an instrumental figure in organizing the Colorado Baseball Partnership's franchise application, but this was no pleasure call. In fact, the franchise Jacobs and countless others had worked so hard to land was in crisis.

Ever since that monumental day in June of 1991, when Major League Baseball's expansion committee announced its decision to award franchises to Denver and South Florida, there had been signs of financial strain in the Rockies' disparate ownership group—enough that MLB officials were losing patience.

"At one point, we had come back from meetings in New York and they were about at the end of their rope with Denver, and were about ready to go with Tampa Bay," McMorris said. "I was told that we had to step up and get this solved, or they would have to make a decision."

And now, this bombshell dropped: Managing general partner Mickey Monus had been charged by federal officials with defrauding $400 million from his Phar-Mor drug store chain. Monus was going down, putting another partner, John Antonucci, in financial jeopardy.

The Brain Trust: Jerry McMorris, left, and Bob Gebhard in 1996. *AP Images*

The franchise was hemorrhaging at the top, and an immediate solution was needed.

"It definitely was a crisis moment," McMorris said. "That's when we said, 'Let's get the local owners together, and see if we can't come up with a solution.' And we did."

Baseball fans in the Rocky Mountain region should be forever grateful.

Up to that point, the Colorado investors were limited partners. None of them wanted the management responsibility that went along with being the general partner, Monus' position. That included McMorris, a trucker by trade with no baseball experience other than playing in his youth. But now it was obvious that if the franchise was to be salvaged, the locals had to do it.

"The governor asked me to step up and show some leadership,"

McMorris said. "And none of us—I'm talking about Charlie Monfort, Oren Benton, and Pete Coors—wanted to see the franchise get away. We thought getting Major League Baseball to Denver was good for all the right reasons. And clearly, the community wanted it."

At that point, the Rockies already had sold 24,000-plus season tickets for the 1993 season. They had signed local radio and television contracts, chosen Tucson, Arizona, as their spring training home, conducted a June draft of amateur talent, and had even laid the groundwork for a new stadium.

The local owners stepped up, covered the shortfall for the $95-million franchise (plus $20-30 million in startup costs), and the Rockies were saved. Monus eventually went to federal prison, and only a few weeks before the inaugural spring training, Antonucci was let go due to a personality and management style clash with McMorris.

And so, ready or not, McMorris stepped into the role of chairman, president, and chief executive officer. The only experienced baseball person he had to lean on was senior vice president/general manager Bob Gebhard.

"Geb was hired by Antonucci, and I was comfortable with that," McMorris said. "We already were so far down the road, and I didn't know much about baseball at that point. The dumbest thing I could do was have to have 'my guy' here running the operation. History says keeping Geb was the right thing to do."

Screams it, actually.

ALL FOR THE ROCKIES

You don't go from expansion infant to playoff qualifier in three seasons without a myriad of things going right.

Unlike previous expansion drafts, the Rockies and Florida Marlins got the benefit of selecting players from all 26 existing teams, as opposed to only one league. They also were able to sign free agents.

Unprecedented record-setting attendance brought in revenue that nobody in the Rockies organization had imagined, and after the painful 1994 strike, Commissioner Bud Selig cooperated by instituting an expanded playoff format of eight teams. But there is little debating the fact that the man behind it all when it came to the Rockies' early success was Gebhard. A tireless worker, he had his hand in everything from scouting and player development to ballpark aesthetics.

Those water fountains and evergreen trees adorning the bullpens and center-field area at Coors Field? They were Gebhard's idea. The policy of having players who signed huge long-term contracts donate money to build area youth-league fields? Gebhard's idea. He made the call on everything from signing Andres Galarraga as a bargain-basement free agent to stealing Curtis Leskanic late in the expansion draft.

"Geb was the catalyst," McMorris said. "He was the face of the organization. He was strong-willed, but he needed to be. He did an unbelievable job putting everything together."

Gebhard was everywhere, usually with a cigarette or cup of coffee in hand. Nobody gave more. A former big-league pitcher, he turned out to be better at building a franchise than he was on the mound. But he never strayed far from the thinking of an old-school scout, and he wasn't the easiest guy to work for, whether you wore a uniform or a tie at the ballpark.

"One time in Chicago, I had pitched a really good game," Leskanic said. "I went into the seventh inning, and the leadoff guy, Sammy Sosa, hit the first pitch off the foul pole for a home run. We were winning 4-0 before that home run, and I remember going up to the clubhouse after I was taken out, and Geb saying to me, 'That's what happens when you get the damn ball up.'

"I was thinking, I just pitched seven innings of two-hit ball, gave up one run—that was pretty good. And here's Geb coming in and saying that. That was his way of saying, 'Good job, but don't be satisfied until you throw nine.' He would always come to my locker and talk to me, get in my ear. I never realized until later that he was just trying to help. He was the best general manager I had in my time in the big leagues. He was all about business. He wanted to win."

Tony Siegle had been in baseball 30 years when he joined the

Rockies as Gebhard's assistant in 1995. But sometimes, Siegle had to wonder if he was an intern.

"Geb wasn't a particularly good delegator," Siegle said with a laugh. "I was as experienced as he was, and yet he would give me an assignment, and tell me how to do it. I'd say, 'Geb, I didn't just fall off the turnip truck. I know how to do this.' He was very hands-on. The reverence I have for that man . . . that S.O.B. was all Rockies, boy. And that was important for the rest of us to remember. Because when we wanted to kill him, we realized it was all for the Rockies."

ARMS RACE

How do you build an organization from the ground up? In Gebhard's mind, there was only one way to go. As a former big-league pitcher, he had a pitching-first mind-set. And since he had seen baseball at high altitude during his days with the Montreal Expos, Gebhard knew he couldn't have enough arms in his organization.

So in the months leading up to the June 1992 amateur draft and the expansion draft five months later, Gebhard and his skeleton crew of a scouting staff concentrated on preparing draft lists full of pitchers.

"The first guy I hired was (scouting director) Pat Daugherty, then (assistant general manager) Randy Smith," Gebhard said. "Once the (1991) World Series was over and I got out to Denver, Pat and I knew it was time to hire scouts. So I went to John Antonucci and asked him, 'What's our budget?' And he told me $300,000 for the entire scouting department. Pat obviously couldn't hire experienced scouts because they were making too much money. So he got assistant coaches at colleges, younger guys, and he put together a 10-man staff.

"He also wanted to hire one experienced guy, Herb Hippauf. So I had to go back to John and get a few extra dollars, and we hired Herb. So Pat, Herb, and 10 rookie scouts, with no follow lists, no experience, nothing, went out and started getting ready for the 1992 draft, of which nine players played in the Major Leagues. I can't say enough about the tremendous job Pat did—and Randy, in helping him. We knew pitchers were the hardest thing to find. I also suspected when clubs turned in their protected lists for the expansion draft, they would protect pitchers. So we went heavy on pitchers in both drafts."

ON A BEND-ER

True to the plan, the Rockies' first amateur draft was littered with arms. The first four selections were college right-handers, and half of the 40 signings were pitchers. For the most part, this first group of Rockies landed together with the organization's primary farm team, the Bend (Oregon) Rockies of the Class-A Northwest League.

From day one, they weren't just a bunch of no-name Minor Leaguers. Not when a baseball-starved Denver area was desperate for a team to cheer for—even if it was a rookie-ball squad over 1,000 miles away.

Between the amateur draft and the June 16 season opener, the Bend players were brought to Denver for a week of workouts, and it was almost like they were the big-league Rockies. Print and television media covered the practices, crowds gathered, and this group of mostly college-age players realized things were different now.

"It was unique," said Mark Strittmatter, a catcher on the Bend team who is now the Rockies' bullpen catcher. "We were all in pro ball for the first time, and there were cameras and reporters everywhere. We weren't expecting anything like that."

From Denver, the frenzy shifted to Bend. The Denver media horde arrived several days early—19 in all were on hand for the opener—and the stands at Vince Genna Stadium were packed with 3,125 fans, as well as the Rockies' brass.

And as it turned out, after falling behind 5-0, the Bend Rockies rallied, with catcher Will Scalzitti—a sixth-round draft choice from Miami-Dade Community College—hitting a grand slam to cap a five-run eighth inning in a come-from-behind 6-5 win over Boise.

"It wasn't the shot heard round the world, but it was a special moment for the organization," pitcher Roger Bailey said. "More than probably any other minor-league team out there, Bend was something special. To this day, that was the best draft the Rockies ever had. That was something for them to brag about. Bob Gebhard, Pat Daugherty—all those guys in the front office did a great job putting that team together, and I think they were proud of us."

The nine players from that 1992 Bend team who eventually reached the Major Leagues were pitchers Juan Acevedo, Garvin Alston, Bailey, John Burke, and Mark Thompson, infielders Jason Bates and Craig Counsell, and outfielders Angel Echevarria and Quinton McCracken. Not surprisingly, there was a division championship in the picture that summer, as Bend won the Southern Division before losing to Bellingham in the championship series.

"Joe Niekro was our pitching coach," Bailey said. "Gene Glynn was our manager. Amos Otis was our hitting coach. Larry Bearnarth had already been named the Rockies pitching coach, and he came out a few times. So we had a major-league staff with us. We had a face-to-face meeting with Bob Gebhard and Jerry McMorris on day one. It was special because we were treated like men. It was shocking at that level. We were treated like major-league guys."

YOU CAN PREVENT FOREST FIRES

While they were treated like men and big-leaguers, those 1992 Bend Rockies were 19-22-year-old kids. Which meant, at times, that they acted like 19-22-year-old kids.

"We almost set a national forest on fire one night," Bailey said. "Or at least we thought we did. We went out after a day game, with no game the next day. There were about a half-dozen of us, and our fianceés were there, too. John Burke was like Paul Bunyan, the great outdoorsman. Coming from Colorado, he had hunted, done all this stuff, so he led the way.

"First, we stole some wood out of somebody's yard. We were still kids, still doing stupid stuff. Then we went out in the woods, built a little fire, had a few beers. We thought we had put out the fire, but when we came back home and turned on the television, there was a story about a fire a couple miles from where we were at, and the National Guard was sent to put it out. So we thought we had something to do with it.

"We called the newspaper and said, 'Hey, we think we might have done something wrong.' For about a three-day stretch, we thought we were responsible, and about 2,500 acres were burned. But as it turned out, we weren't responsible. It was lightning. But we were honest with it. We wanted people to know this wasn't arson or something like that."

IT'S A GROOVE THING

The idea first dawned on Gebhard during the Minnesota Twins' run to a 1987 World Series title. Late in that season, the Twins added Don Baylor to their roster, the kind of quality veteran hitter contenders turn to down the stretch for clutch at-bats.

Baylor's record was well-established—1979 American League MVP and a man so tough that he was the Majors' all-time leader in getting hit by pitches, in part because he wouldn't give ground and back off the plate. What Gebhard learned during that stretch run was the immense leadership skills of the man known around the game as "Groove."

"I told myself then that if I was ever in a position to do so, I wanted to give Don Baylor a chance at managing," Gebhard said.

Five years later, that's exactly what occurred. But not until Gebhard had wrestled with the decision from among four quality candidates: Baylor, the only one with no managing experience—not even in the minors; Bill Virdon, an older, established big-league manager and disciplinarian known for his patience; Tony Muser, a veteran baseball man who had managed the Triple-A Denver Zephyrs; and Tom Trebelhorn, another experienced big-league skipper regarded as a sound teacher of the game's fundamentals.

"We brought in those four guys," Gebhard said. "Jerry McMorris sat in. John Antonucci sat in there. And John McHale Jr. and I did the interviews. I'll never forget, Jerry, as we walked out, said, 'All four of these guys are good.'

"The next day, I said, 'Unless somebody has a problem, Don Baylor is going to be the guy. I think Don has a high ceiling, and I want to give him an opportunity.' He brought a presence to us. Don said in his very first press conference, 'Everybody is going to expect us to lose 100 games, but it's not going to happen.' And it didn't."

Baylor had interviewed for managerial positions in Milwaukee and Seattle, and was serving as Joe Torre's hitting coach in St. Louis when the call came from Gebhard.

"Working for Joe prepared me for the Colorado job," Baylor said. "What patience I had, I saw it with Joe. Geb gave me an opportunity, and I'll always thank him for that. Nobody else did at the time. Seattle took Bill Plummer instead, and I think he made it through one year. I thought that was going to be the job for me. At the time, the only guy I knew who was connected with the Rockies was (*Rocky Mountain News* baseball writer) Tracy Ringolsby. I called him to get an idea about the people in the organization. I was interviewing for a job that didn't have major-league players."

A DRAFT FOR THE AGES

If the passage of time is the best way to judge the 1992 expansion draft, then enough has gone by to make a clear assessment: the Rockies rocked. If there is another expansion draft in Major League baseball's future, the participants will have a hard time matching what Gebhard and staff pulled off on November 17 in the Marriott Marquis Hotel in New York.

As about 20,000 people gathered in a downtown Denver convention hall to watch along with a national cable television audience, names that would become Rockies anchors were plucked from teams that figured they were expendable.

Vinny Castilla. Eric Young. Steve Reed. Kevin Ritz. Charlie Hayes. Darren Holmes. Joe Girardi. Armando Reynoso. David Nied. Kevin Reimer turned into Dante Bichette with the completion of a draft-day trade. Then-prospects Brad Ausmus and Andy Ashby would be part of an infamous trade in the summer of 1993 on their way to productive big-league careers.

All were gobbled up by the Rockies among the 72 players selected. Nied was the first overall pick, Hayes was a second-round steal, and

Gebhard saved some beauties for late—Ausmus, Reynoso, Reed, and Leskanic—the 66th name called that day.

The talent haul was the culmination of thousands of man hours logged by Gebhard, Bearnarth, Smith, and Daugherty's young scouts. But money—or lack thereof—had an influence as well.

"Four or five weeks before the draft, I was told that I only had $8 million for our 40-man roster for the 1993 season," Gebhard said. "I thought about it for a while, and I realized that was information I couldn't share with anybody—not even our manager and coaches—because if it got out, it would affect how the other clubs would decide on protecting their players, who they would pull back, etc. Florida pretty much had an open checkbook. We had to do our research on the players we liked, and estimate what they might earn in 1993. We went to New York and did the draft, and John McHale had his calculator, adding up salaries as we picked guys."

HI, MY NAME IS . . .

The expansion draft was in the books, free agents Galarraga, Bryn Smith, and Bruce Ruffin had been signed, Bichette and Rudy Seanez had come in trades, and ready or not, it was time for the first spring training for the first team from the Mountain Time zone.

Tucson was the gathering spot, and at that time the Rockies' camp was isolated from the rest of the Cactus League's teams based in the Phoenix area, which would prove to be a logistical nightmare once the exhibition games began.

But a more immediate concern arose. If you looked around the home clubhouse at Hi Corbett Field, you could find an equipment travel bag from virtually every other major-league club. Everybody had come from somewhere else, and nobody knew who anybody else was.

"It was like misfit island," Leskanic said. "All these guys were there in the locker room and you looked around and thought, this team

Eric Young's 1993 Opening Day lead-off homer remains one of the franchise's greatest moments. *AP Images*

didn't want this guy, that team didn't protect that guy. Nobody wanted these guys. They were just cast aside."

But a solution wasn't long in coming.

"I want to say we had 68-69 players in camp, and we didn't have a lot of veteran presence," said Mike Swanson, the club's media relations director for six seasons. "Bryn Smith not only was a veteran, but was a very humorous, very well-intentioned, creative veteran.

"We had very generic spring training jerseys, with no names on the back. During the first team meeting, Smitty came up to me and said, 'We need name tags.' I laughed at first, but then I thought, you know what, he's not laughing. He's serious. So we sent 'Tucson Lenny' to get some.

"Anything you needed in Tucson, Lenny could get it. He drove an old, beat-up convertible covered in bumper stickers, wore crazy outfits, had that never-smoked, foot-long cigar hanging out of his mouth. He was a character. Lenny Rubin was his full name.

"So I told Lenny, 'We need you to go to Target or Wal-Mart, and get those, "Hi, my name is . . ." tags.'

"And he said, 'For what? Are we having a dinner?'

"And I said, 'Just trust me. Go get them.'

"He came back with them, put them in Smitty's locker, and after the workout, Smitty told everybody they had to fill them out.

"The next day, every player walked on the field with a name tag. Don Baylor was trying his best to be the intimidating soul he can be. This was his first managerial gig, and he wanted to let everybody know he was in an authority role. I don't know how much he wanted to laugh right out of the shoot, but he gut-laughed with that one. Guys were doing their stretching, exercising, running, hitting until those things just fell off."

OPENING DAY I

Eventually, everybody learned everybody else's name, and Baylor and his coaching staff put together a starting lineup, a rotation, a bullpen, and a bench. It wasn't much to threaten the National League with, but it was all they had.

No bigger example of that was Baylor's choice for the Opening Day starter. David Nied had pitched all of 23 major-league innings when he got the assignment. They were an impressive 23 innings—3-0 with a 1.17 ERA and only 10 hits allowed. But he was a 24-year-old kid—a humble, well-mannered one—who had no business being at the front end of a big-league rotation at that point.

If they had been able to keep Nied in Atlanta, you could have envisioned Bobby Cox breaking him in slowly in middle relief, maybe even giving him a spot start or two. But Nied wasn't going to crack the Braves foursome of Greg Maddux, Tom Glavine, John Smoltz, and Steve Avery, so he was left unprotected, and the Rockies grabbed him before the Marlins could.

On expansion-draft day, Nied got an inkling of what was to come when he was introduced to a manic crowd of about 20,000 gathered at a downtown Denver convention hall to watch the proceedings.

"I've never had an adrenaline rush like that," he said at the time. "Not when I was on the World Series roster with the Braves. Never."

And sure enough, the role of No. 1 starter proved to be too much for him. By May, he twice had avoided media interviews and complained about the unfairness of pitching at a high altitude. By June, he landed on the disabled list with elbow problems, already beaten down emotionally and physically.

Yet there was Nied on Opening Day—April 5, 1993, before 53,134 fans at Shea Stadium—going against Dwight Gooden. The result was predictable: a 3-0 Mets victory, with Nied surrendering a home run to Bobby Bonilla and tentatively making his way through five innings.

The rest of the Rockies' lineup read: second baseman Eric Young; center fielder Alex Cole; right fielder Dante Bichette; first baseman Andres Galarraga; left fielder Jerald Clark; third baseman Charlie Hayes; catcher Joe Girardi; and shortstop Freddy Benavides. That lineup remains etched in Baylor's muscle memory as he wrote out more than 30 lineup cards that day, one for every player and coach.

"You're only going to have one of those . . . Opening Day to start a franchise," Baylor said.

OPENING DAY II

Never mind the 0-2 beginning and .102 team batting average in New York. The Rockies were coming home, and Denver was in an uproar. About 20,000 people gathered for a downtown parade on the day before the first home game in franchise history. About 5,000 made their way to Mile High Stadium for the team's workout that afternoon.

Seventeen months down the road, labor strife would shut down the game. Eventually fan interest in the Rockies would wane. The team would flounder, and the losing seasons would pile up. But on April 8, 1993, the Rockies were a newborn being celebrated with exuberance that bordered on the irrational.

As Baylor entered the stadium that morning, he saw workers erecting temporary bleachers to help accommodate what would be a major league-record crowd of 80,227. Someone even penned a take-off on "Twas the Night Before Christmas," complete with a mention of every player and coach. A portion of it, as it appeared in *They've Got Rockies In Their Heads* by Lew Cady (1993, Mile High Press):

With a crafty, sly manager, a man on the move,
I knew in a moment it had to be Groove

More rapid than eagles, his runners they came
And he whistled and shouted and called them by name:

Now Dante! Now Alex! Now Freddie and Andres
On Darren! On Jerald! On, Joey and Hayes!

The Rockies' home opener went into the books as an 11-4 victory over the Montreal Expos, but it wasn't just a game, it was an experience. There would be 18 Rockies hits and seven shutout innings from Smith,

---

Injuries shortened David Nied's career after he was the first pick in the 1992 expansion draft. *AP Images*

but one moment mattered most, and still does in the hearts and minds of many Rockies fans:

Bottom of the first inning, Kent Bottenfield—who later that season would wear a Rockies uniform—on the mound, leadoff hitter Young at the plate. Talk about your first impressions . . . at precisely 3:17 p.m., Young belted a 3-2 pitch over the left-center field fence to create a moment that words can barely do justice.

At the time, third-base coach Don Zimmer said: "I'm a 62-year-old man who has been in this game for 44 years, and when he hit that home run, I had chills running up and down my spine."

So did Mike Klis, who covered the event for the *Colorado Springs Gazette-Telegraph.*

"I've said this: if the Rockies ever win the World Series, I would be willing to at least discuss that Opening Day in 1993 was bigger," he said. "That was unbelievable. 80,227 fans . . . the electricity in that place. When E.Y. hit that home run, it was the most spine-tingling moment in anything I've ever covered."

Baylor couldn't help but remember what he had told Young after his first at-bat in New York a few days earlier, when Young tried unsuccessfully to bunt for a base hit as the first batter in franchise history.

"I told him, 'You're leading off the organization, and you try to bunt for a hit?' I wanted to see him swing the bat in that spot. You want to see a clean single or double to start the franchise off.

"So then we go back home, and how could you draw that up? You couldn't do it. That was just incredible. Everybody was excited about that game. It was a dramatic day. E.Y. hits the home run, and you know that's a game you want to win. You have to win that game."

And from the little big man himself:

"I remember Groove telling me about that bunt (attempt in New York)," Young said. "After the home run, I should have said, 'Is that what you wanted me to do?' I felt like I was floating when I was running around the bases—like my feet weren't even touching the ground. I had chills running through my body, and I remember it felt like the stadium was shaking."

DOUBTING THOMAS

Early in the 1993 season, few believed in the staying power of the attendance phenomenon going on in the Rockies. One of the doubters was Gebhard's friend in the Twins organization.

"A good friend of mine worked in the ticket department in Minnesota, and when I first came out here, we talked back and forth," Gebhard said. "In spring training, he asked me, 'Are you going to draw any people out there in the mountains?'

"And I told him, 'We're going to try to set a new attendance record and draw 80,000 on Opening Day,' and he laughed and laughed.

"So we get to the first game, and I called him about the third inning, and I told him, 'We made it.'

"And he said, 'What are you talking about?'

"I said, 'We've got over 80,000 here. Read the paper tomorrow.'

"And he said, 'Yeah, Opening Day . . . tomorrow you'll have about 10,000.'

"I called him back the next day, and I said, 'Well, you were right; the attendance did drop.'

"And he said, 'How many do you have?'

"And I said, 'We're down to about 63,000.' And every day, it was like that."

FANDEMONIUM

Crowds of 80,000 weren't everyday occurrences, but with more than 28,000 season tickets sold, the Rockies had 2.2 million in guaranteed attendance before the first pitch was thrown on Opening Day.

With a regional fan base and huge daily walkup totals, attendance records started falling—11 in all that season. It took only 17 home dates to cross the one-million mark.

The two-million mark was surpassed on Fathers' Day, again the fastest in history. In between—home game No. 30, to be precise—they surpassed the single-season record for an expansion team, previously held by the 1977 Toronto Blue Jays. On and on it went, homestand after homestand.

"I remember pretty early that season, we played Philadelphia," Gebhard said. "We weren't very good, and they were. They went to the World Series that year. And they were beating us bad, 18-0, I think.

"It's real late in the game, and we finally get a run to make it a real lot-to-1. And everybody went nuts. You'd think we had just won the World Series. I looked out into the parking lot, and all the cars were still there. Nobody was leaving."

The three-million mark was passed on July 28, in the 53rd home game. The single-season National League record fell on August 30. The *smallest* crowd of the season was 40,814 on September 15 against Houston. Two days later, the all-time single-season record was established, passing the 1992 Blue Jays.

It was part of Swanson's duties to make the daily attendance announcements to press box inhabitants.

"I'd think to myself, 'I didn't just get on the PA and say 'Tonight's attendance is 67,485. That brings the season total to 3,400,000,' did I?" he said. "When we got over the four-million mark, it was absolutely mind-boggling."

In the end, the Rockies would smash the previous record by more than 300,000, and finish with an incredible 4,485,350 fans—still the most in major-league history. The average crowd was 56,751 for 79 dates—there were two rainouts—with nine crowds of 70,000-plus and 27 crowds of 60,000-plus.

"All the hoopla and excitement made it so much fun," Bichette said. "It was a once-in-a-lifetime deal. It was electric. We were on top of the world. It was different than anything else I experienced in the Major Leagues. When I played in Boston later in my career, the Red Sox-Yankees rivalry was intense. But this was more like a celebration."

A WALK IN THE PARK

Not that it mattered much to the fans, but there was an expansion team on the field in 1993, and that meant massive roster changes and too many losses.

Dale Murphy retired in late May after a failed stint as a pinch-hitter.

Smith was released on June 2 with an 8.49 ERA. Young moved from second base to left field to replace Clark and make room for rookie Roberto Mejia. The rotation that started the season had entirely changed by the All-Star break.

There was a demoralizing 13-game losing streak in late July/early August, and then an uplifting finish behind a streaking bullpen—a 17-9 September that marked the first winning final month for an expansion team.

The Rockies got that important 63rd victory—the one that meant they wouldn't lose 100 games—on the second-to-last home game, and in the home finale, Young hit not one but two homers, his first since Opening Day.

After that final home game, it was Baylor's idea for his team to take a lap around the field, players and coaches circling the entire warning track, stopping to talk to fans, and saying thank you. The love affair between the Rockies and their fans had another memorable moment.

"The lap? It hadn't been done before, not that I know of," Baylor said. "It was something we felt we had to do, something I felt I had to do. To say thanks—80,227 the first day, four million-plus—was unique."

The first-year Rockies finished 67-95—the third-best record among the game's 12 expansion teams at that point, and good enough for sixth place in the seven-team National League West.

"I grew up with the (Houston) Colt 45's when they first started, watching those games and seeing loss after loss," Baylor said. "People were saying, 'Oh, expansion teams always lose 100 games.' That always stuck in my craw.

"And then here I was, managing an expansion team that should lose 100 games. But I said, 'It's not going to happen.' We got into that losing streak. . . . Man oh man, you'd almost give up your first born for a win. But we didn't lose 100."

MILE HIGH SALUTE

There was no victory lap around Mile High after the final home game of the 1994 season. That's because nobody knew that an embarrassing loss on August 11 to the Atlanta Braves would be the last game the Rockies played that year. The next day, the players union went on strike, and there wasn't another pitch thrown.

So the last game in Mile High went down as one of the worst—a 13-0 whitewashing featuring 20 Braves hits and four Rockies errors. Maddux got as many hits at the plate as he allowed in a complete-game victory (three), and lowered his ERA to 1.56 on the way to the third of four consecutive Cy Young Awards.

"The whole day was surreal," Weiss said. "Maddux mowed us down. I think one ball left the infield. When I went to the Braves in 1998 and talked to Maddux about it, he said, 'You guys weren't trying that day. You were already on strike.' I don't think that was the case, but the whole day was weird. It was more about what was going to happen after the game. The game was almost secondary."

In 56 games played at Mile High Stadium in 1994, the Rockies drew 3,281,511 fans, or an average of 58,598—which, believe it or not, was more than they had averaged per game in 1993. A full season would have given them another single-season attendance record. Instead, their 1993 total of 4,485,350 fans still stands.

The legacy left by Mile High is now felt at Coors Field, which was expanded from its original plan of about 41,000 seats. Because of the overwhelming fan support, the club footed the bill to increase Coors Field's capacity to 50,449 by adding the right-field upper deck, and for a handful of years, even that wasn't enough to meet the demand.

"We knew that decision had some risk, that the day might come when we couldn't sell all those seats," McMorris said. "But at the time, the kind of support we had made it seem like the right decision. The (extra) seats paid for themselves, many times."

3

1995: A MAGICAL TIME

IMPECCABLE TIMING

In Rockies history, 1995 stands as a testament to the uncommon fortitude of a special group of relievers, the overwhelming support of a rabid fan base in a beautiful state-of-the-art ballpark, and the realization that there is a first time for everything.

It was a season when a slugging David unexpectedly slew the pitching-and-defense Goliaths, and the baby of a franchise reached the playoffs in its third season, despite (and because of) the game-altering affects of mile-high altitude and thin, dry air.

"Catching Wildcard Fever" screamed the headline atop the *Denver Post*'s sports section on October 2, 1995—the day after the Rockies clinched their first playoff spot—and it would take another 12 years for them to get back to the postseason.

"Those really were magic times," Siegle said. "It was a love affair. We opened the doors and people filled the seats. That town came alive in 1995. I've never seen anything like it in 42 years in baseball. It did wonders for that city, for that area. It was fun to go to that ballpark. I was proud to work there."

An unlikely alignment of variables made it possible, starting with record-smashing attendance that facilitated a payroll expansion from $8 million in 1993 to more than three times that in 1995.

There was a mix of emerging young talent (Young, Castilla), solid, role-playing veterans (Weiss, Girardi, Mike Kingery), middle-of-the-lineup mashers who came relatively cheap due to earlier career valleys (Bichette, Galarraga, Ellis Burks) and one superstar in the making (Larry Walker). In today's market, that collection of talent would form an unwieldy $100-million-plus payroll, well beyond the Rockies' means. But in 1995, it was the perfect mix at the perfect time.

With so many class-act veterans, the clubhouse was a harmonious place, the chemistry transferred to the diamond, and an undeniable comeback mentality took root at Coors Field.

Even the labor strife that severely damaged the game at that time worked in the Rockies' favor. The 144-game season spared their stretched-to-the-limit bullpen, and the baseball honeymoon went on unabated, unlike the ugliness occurring in ballparks around the country.

"All the moons were aligned," Weiss said. "The timing of it all was impeccable."

REPLACEABLE PARTS

Before there were the actual 1995 Rockies, who reached postseason play faster than any other expansion franchise, there were the Replacement Rockies. They were polite, humble, and grateful for the opportunity they received to live out their dreams, even if it was only for a little while.

But striking players, the media, and even Baylor were united against the idea of fielding a replacement team. *Denver Post* columnist Woody Paige wrote, "Nobody in Denver wants to watch the Colorado Scabbies play the St. Louis DisCards or the Philadelphia Phonies." Pitcher Marvin Freeman told a reporter, "Get ready to laugh" at the prospect of replacement-player games. And union activist Girardi went so far as to bite the hand that had fed him a three-year, $5-million deal by accusing Rockies management of bribing minor-leaguers with offers of $150 per game to play in replacement exhibition games.

But the worst fears were realized, fittingly enough on April 1, when a brand-new Coors Field was christened by a 7-6 Replacement Rockies

Coors Field, shown here on March 31, 1995, and remains one of the game's most beautiful ballparks. *AP Images*

victory over the New York Replacement Yankees.

"What a terrible way to break in a new stadium," Siegle said. "The first replacement player game was bizarre and surreal, with players most of whom we'd never heard of playing at Coors Field, and we were calling it a major-league game."

It was a time Baylor would rather forget.

"You walk into Coors Field through the left-field gate, and here's this pristine ballpark," Baylor said. "And then these players walk into the clubhouse and their names are on their lockers. They were all excited. They had those throwaway cameras, taking pictures. I was thinking, 'Let me get my keys and get the hell out of here.'"

For what it was worth, the Rockies put together one of the better replacement teams—one that featured former major-league pitchers Jeff Sellers and Lee Tunnell, a handful of solid organization players, and a bunch of guys never heard of before or since, led by starting pitcher Albert Bustillos.

"We worked hard at it," Siegle said. "There were four of us out signing players and trying to coerce, for lack of a better word, some of our minor-leaguers to play. Poor Angel Echevarria. He did it because his mom was dying of cancer and needed the money for surgery. But Trent Hubbard, he was on the brink and didn't. That was the weirdest time."

Truth be told, there was one other important aspect to the Coors Field replacement games:

"We were going to use an artist's concept for the cover of the media guide that year," Swanson said. "But then we had the replacement games with the Yankees, and we sent a plane airborne with a photographer, and he took a picture of a full Coors Field.

"We had a hold on the media guide because when the strike was over, we were going to sign Larry Walker and Bill Swift, and I had to have them in the guide. So that picture got on the cover. It's a beautiful aerial shot of a full house at Coors Field, but the little specks on the field are replacement players. It's not Dante. It's not Larry Walker. It's Ben Ortman and those other guys."

GOOD VIBRATIONS

The real Rockies couldn't wait for the shortened 1995 season to begin, and unlike other places around the Majors, neither could their fans. The combination of a focused team drawing so many fans with a beautiful new ballpark was undoubtedly a factor in the unexpected run to the playoffs.

Baseball took a major hit with the 1994 strike and spring 1995 replacement games. The Montreal Expos franchise never recovered financially, and eventually moved to Washington. Even in a baseball Mecca like St. Louis, post-strike fan rancor could be heard and felt around Busch Stadium. Meanwhile, the honeymoon continued in Denver.

"Once the strike was settled, it was business as usual for us," Bichette said. "We didn't have a lot of animosities built up, like in some of the

Walt Weiss, now in the front office, was a gifted defensive shortstop and valued team leader. *AP Images*

other cities. Everything was still exciting for us. We were moving into a new park. I think that helped the team. And as a team, we worked hard to make it that way. We wanted to play ball."

Weiss compared the atmosphere around the Rockies to the togetherness of a college team.

"We really were a close-knit group," he said. "It's very rare that you have team chemistry first, and then you win. Usually, winning creates the chemistry. But this was a unique group of guys. We had some characters, and the fans loved us. We knew it was fun at the time, but you don't realize how unique it was until you look back on it years later."

Added Siegle: "I've always said that a team's makeup is just as important as the talent. That club had both. When they went on the field, it was like a Swiss watch. They played hard every day, and that means something, because it becomes contagious. It was a wonderfully constructed club."

OH WHAT A NIGHT!

It stretched 14 innings—four hours and 49 minutes. There were 20 runs scored, 33 hits and four ties. Snow blanketed the ballpark when players and coaches arrived late that morning. The official box score temperature read 42 degrees, but it was nowhere near that by the time the game ended.

But the lasting memory from the first real Opening Day at Coors Field was one swing of the bat by Bichette that ended a game and set the tone for an entire season. What started as a late-afternoon game had turned into a night game when Bichette connected off left-hander Mike Remlinger, setting off jubilation around the park when the ball landed in the left-field seats.

"I consider it my career highlight," Bichette said. "Especially because of the way my off-season went. I wasn't signed until the last minute that spring. They had signed Larry (Walker). I was promised a deal, but was just left out there for a long time during spring training. Finally, Don called me and said, 'I want you here.' And it finally got done. So there were some pent-up feelings involved.

"It was electric that day, really exciting. It was a seesaw game, and it just kept going and going. Remlinger hung a changeup, and I got it. The fist-pump to the guys (in the dugout), that was just true emotion. When I got to the dugout, I ran all the way up to the clubhouse. I beat everybody there. I just had to run somewhere. I was so psyched."

Bichette's Opening Day walkoff homer was just the beginning. There was no such thing as a safe lead in Coors Field, and more often than not, it was the Rockies doing the late rallying to victory.

"When Dante hit that home run and fist-pumped to the dugout, it was like, 'We'll be damned if anybody is going to come in here and kick our ass,'" Leskanic said. "If you look at our record at home, that's just the way it was."

At home, the Rockies were a dominating 44-28. While on the road, they barely held their own at 33-39, a recurring pattern throughout their history.

"They started believing, and then it had a life of its own," Baylor said. "We just didn't want to give up. The ballpark definitely helped. The difference between Mile High and Coors Field was that at Coors Field, the fans were right there on top of you. You could feel the vibration. We had crowds of 70,000 five or six times at Mile High, but it didn't feel like the 50,000 in Coors Field."

STANDING ROOM ONLY

Not long into the 1995 season, Rockies fans began a consecutive sellout streak at Coors Field that would stretch 203 games—from June 13, 1995 to September 5, 1997. Not coincidentally, the Rockies' record in those games was an impressive 127-76, or a .626 winning percentage.

For a long while, the Cleveland Indians' streak at Jacobs Field ran concurrent with the one at Coors Field, and they eventually set a major-league record at 455 in a row. All of which led to an ongoing rivalry between Swanson and his media-relations cohort in Cleveland: Bart Swain.

"Poor Bart. They'd start their games an hour earlier than ours, and Bart would call and say, 'We're sold out, what do you have tonight?'" Swanson said. "And I'd say, 'We're sold out, too.' And Bart would say, 'Nooo . . .' He was hoping our streak would end, I was hoping theirs would end."

IT WAS THE THOUGHT THAT COUNTED

The Rockies unexpectedly found themselves in first place at the All-Star break, despite pitching staff upheaval. Ruffin and Nied were on the disabled list. Omar Olivares had been released. The closer role was undefined. And as the trade deadline approached, Freeman—already suffering through an ineffective season—strained his oblique muscle in a start against San Francisco. Swift and Joe Grahe had shoulders that were acting up, too.

So that's when Gebhard pulled the trigger on a deal for Bret Saberhagen, sending pitching prospects Acevedo and Arnold Gooch to the New York Mets. In the minds of the Rockies players, who found out on a team flight back from Montreal, this was the last piece to their playoff puzzle. It was as if Christmas had come early.

"We felt like we were one starter away from being the team to beat," Bichette recalled. "Then we made the trade for Sabes, and we felt like we had our guy. I remember the whole plane got crazy. Everybody went nuts."

It wasn't so much what Saberhagen did over the rest of that season. In fact, he made only three starts before shoulder trouble resurfaced and bothered him the rest of the way. In nine starts, he was 2-1 with a 6.28 ERA and 60 hits and 13 walks allowed in 40 innings.

But his presence helped the team get over the hump mentally. His 139 career wins, two Cy Young Awards, and a World Series MVP award were reasons to believe that a team in its third year could reach the postseason.

"To get a marquee guy like that, right before the deadline, talk about a shot in the arm," Weiss said. "Unfortunately, we didn't see the real Bret Saberhagen here.

He took a lot of heat here, but it wasn't his fault. He was hurt. When he went out there and pitched, it was all on guts. We had a lot of respect for him, because we knew what he was dealing with. We know how tough this game is when you're healthy."

Saberhagen made his Rockies debut a few days later—August 3—and it was another of those moments only Coors Field at the time could produce. In 6⅓ innings, he gave up four runs, though it could have been worse, as he surrendered 13 hits and four walks. When Saberhagen walked off the mound with a lead, an unfailingly loyal

Injuries limited Bret Saberhagen's effectiveness, but he provided an emotional lift in 1995.
AP Images

crowd gave him a long standing ovation as if he had just pitched a complete-game shutout.

"I remember him saying afterward, 'That's the first time I got a standing ovation after giving up four runs and 13 hits,'" Gebhard said.

JUMPING FOR JOY

Talk about cutting it close: the standings entering the final day of the 1995 regular season had the Rockies one game behind the first-place Los Angeles Dodgers in the National League West, and one game ahead of the Houston Astros in the wildcard race. And then a worst-case scenario unfolded. A sore-shouldered Saberhagen couldn't make it out of the third inning, and the Rockies trailed San Francisco, 8-2.

"When he came in from the bullpen before that last game, I met him at the water cooler, and he was trembling," Baylor said about Saberhagen. "Here's a guy who had been in a World Series, won a Cy Young, and his hands were trembling.

"It was nerve-wracking for him, knowing that he was hurt, knowing what the fans expected. He went out there, gave it what he had, but it got to the point where I had to go get him. We had to play catch-up. We had to win that day."

Fortunately for the Rockies, the Cubs put a six-spot on the board against the Astros in the bottom of the third at Wrigley Field. It didn't last, though, as the Astros rallied to tie it two innings later and eventually won 8-7, setting up the possibility of a one-game playoff for the wildcard spot, as the Dodgers won to clinch the West.

Back in Coors Field, the Giants' lead evaporated quickly. Young and Walker hit two-run homers off Joe Rosselli to cut the deficit to 8-6. A four-run inning against Mark Leiter—who had ripped the Rockies earlier in the season—gave the Rockies a 10-8 lead.

A Giants run in the seventh made it a one-run game, and it boiled down to the top of the ninth inning and the most important save opportunity of Leskanic's career. With a playoff spot on the line, the excitement was palpable. The place was shaking, and an uproarious crowd was hoping and praying that Leskanic would get the final three outs. What they didn't know was that he had trouble seeing home plate.

"If you play at Coors, you know that a lot of shadows and sun come into effect, especially from the third-base side," Leskanic said. "This was late afternoon, about four o'clock. I remember coming into the game and warming up, and the sun for some reason was beaming right into my face when I'm in the stretch. I'm thinking, 'Where the hell is this light coming from?'

"I got the first two guys out, and then Glenallen Hill got a hit. So the sun is still right in my eyes, and it was really a struggle to see. And at the same time, once there were two outs, the mound was trembling. I could feel the earth, like it was an earthquake.

"I threw a cutter inside on Jeff Reed's hands, and I remember him swinging. I thought, 'Oh, no,' because I didn't see where it went at first. But it was a little broken-bat bouncer to first. 'Cat' (Galaraga) made the play and I remember jumping for joy, like I had just lost my marbles."

GOOD ENOUGH OVER 144 GAMES

The Rockies' 1995 feel-good story wasn't quite as popular in other clubhouses around the country. Cincinnati Reds general manager Jim Bowden compared Coors Field to a pinball machine, and called the game played there "arena baseball." Dodgers first baseman Eric Karros looked at the Rockies' roster filled with veteran players, and said he was tired of hearing "that expansion baseball garbage." The Giants' Leiter said, "The Rockies are so cocky and arrogant, they think they invented the game."

And truth be told, even some of the Rockies admit that if a full 162-game season had been completed—18 more than they played due to the strike—there might not have been a postseason appearance. Their bullpen was so stretched that another 18 games might have done them in.

"We might not have won it if we had played a full season," Siegle said. "Our pitchers' arms were held together with rubber bands, bubble gum, and fly paper. I can still remember how tired they were. I've never had more admiration for a group of kids than that bullpen."

Added Leskanic: "By the end of the season, my arm was practically falling off. At that point, I was just trying to throw it over the plate. Me, Ruffin, Holmie, Reeder, Munoz . . . we all had 70-some appearances, and that was in a shorter season. We weren't well-known at the beginning of that year, but we were household names by the end."

WOULDA, COULDA, SHOULDA

Making the playoffs in their third year of existence? When no other team had done it in fewer than eight? Sure, the rules made it easier for the Rockies than previous expansion franchises. But still . . .

"Getting to the playoffs in three years meant an awful lot to the city, to the community," Gebhard said. "To be able to put it together that fast, and to play as well as we did, was special."

But the Rockies weren't the Atlanta Braves. For starters, they had only three players—Weiss, Burks, and Saberhagen—who had any postseason experience. In contrast, the Braves were in year four of an unparalleled run of 14 consecutive division titles. And there was more bad news: the Braves held a 30-6 lifetime advantage over the Rockies, including an unblemished 13-0 record in 1993.

And yet, the Rockies would lead in all four games of the division series, and could have won two of the three games they lost with a timely hit or two. So close, yet so far away.

"We had our opportunities, that's what I remember," said Bichette, who hit .588 in the series. "We probably should have won the series. We had the right guys up at the right time. We just didn't come through. Anybody but the Braves; they had our number, didn't they? They were all pitching and very clutch. And they were the best defensive team in baseball."

Weiss ended up wearing a Braves uniform three years later, and it was then that he heard what the Braves really thought.

"One of the first things I heard when I walked into their clubhouse was that that was the one series they were really worried about that year," Weiss said. "They wanted no part of us. Smoltz to this day says our lineup was the toughest he's ever faced. That's a strong statement. He's been in the league so many years, and pitched in countless post-season games. They had the best team in the National League, no doubt about it. But they had to come and play in this monster (Coors Field). They had their hands full."

GAME 1

It doesn't quite compare to the ball trickling through Billy Buckner's legs in Game 6 of the 1986 World Series, or even to the

Bartman moment in Game 6 of the 2003 National League Championship Series. But when you make only one playoff appearance in the franchise's first 14 seasons, and the first game of that series ends with Game 2 starting pitcher Lance Painter forced into a pinch-hitting role in the ninth inning, it has to rank as a moment of infamy.

Baylor, who won the National League Manager of the Year award that season, ran out of position players in a nine-inning game, and had to send Painter to the plate in a crucial situation. Painter was overmatched by Mark Wohlers and his 100-mph fastball, and the strikeout ended the game with bases loaded and the Braves winning, 5-4.

"I'd probably do it differently now," Baylor admitted.

The move that sparked the most criticism was Baylor pinch-running for Castilla after a leadoff double in the bottom of the seventh. Speedy Trenidad Hubbard was sent in, in theory so he could beat a potential throw to third base on a sacrifice-bunt attempt.

After No. 8 hitter Weiss was hit by a pitch, the bunt was definitely in order, and pinch-hitter Jason Bates laid it down, but Weiss was forced at second. After Young was intentionally walked to load the bases, pinch-hitter deluxe John Vander Wal got his opportunity in Girardi's spot (which would force another move behind the plate). But Vander Wal, who set a big-league record with 28 pinch-hits that season, bounced into a crushing 1-2-3 inning-ending double play.

Bates stayed in at third base, and Jayhawk Owens replaced Girardi, leaving only Kingery on the bench, but in a double-switch Kingery went into the game in the top of the ninth, coming up second in the bottom of that inning, and singled. The Rockies loaded the bases again, but Wohlers got a huge out by striking out Galarraga, and then the pitcher's spot—originally Castilla's—was left. On came Painter, and there went the Rockies' chances.

"For me, I always thought you had to tie the game before you could win it," Baylor said. "Painter up there against Wohlers? He had never seen anything like that. But Wohlers still had to get him out."

When asked about running out of position players in the ninth inning, Gebhard just shook his head and let Siegle talk:

"That move in the playoffs where (Baylor) pinch-ran for Vinny, we came up facing Wohlers, and we had to pinch-hit Painter? I can't get over that. I think that was a crucial move in that playoff. That play was critical. When it doesn't work, you pay for it."

However, both Baylor and Braves manager Bobby Cox said Game 1 turned in the eighth inning, not the ninth, when Chipper Jones robbed Galarraga of a double down the line with a great stop, and turned it into a forced out at second base, keeping the Braves one run ahead.

"The thing I remember most about that series is Chipper making that play behind the bag," Cox said 12 years after the fact. "I'll never forget it."

What gets Baylor's goat to this day is that Braves bench coach Pat Corrales moved Jones closer to the line just before Galarraga's smash. If he hadn't, the Rockies probably would have taken the lead that inning.

"Right before that, Corrales moved Chipper closer to the line," Baylor said. "He moved him. Cat hits a screamer down there, and Chipper grabbed it. We should have won that game. That changed the momentum completely."

GAME 2

Painter made it through five innings on the night after his fateful pinch-hit appearance, and other than two home runs served up to Marquis Grissom—one on the first pitch of the game—pitched effectively. But Painter was dueling Glavine, which meant effective wasn't good enough. Glavine had tossed a shutout on June 16 at Coors Field, and tacked on five more scoreless frames in this one.

But all of a sudden, Walker got the Rockies back in it with a 442-foot, three-run homer to tie the game at three. Galarraga's double scored Bichette with the temporary go-ahead run in the bottom of the eighth, temporary being the operative word here. Because what followed was a ninth-inning collapse and a 7-4 Rockies loss—four runs allowed, the latter two from when Young threw away a two-out groundball.

Leskanic, showing fatigue from a stretch run of heavy use and maximum effort, gave up a double to Jones. Mike Munoz couldn't get lefty Fred McGriff, whose bloop single scored Jones, to tie it at four. Then Holmes served up a too-fat 3-0 pitch that pinch-hitter Mike Mordecai drilled for a game-deciding RBI single.

"They were dead tired," Baylor said of his relievers. "They all wanted the ball, though. They never turned it down."

GAME 3

After an off day dealing with the effects of Hurricane Opal, the Rockies resumed an attempt at the impossible in Atlanta. No team had lost the first two games of a five-game postseason series at home and come back to win the series. And it wasn't going to happen this time, either.

But there would be no sweep, and it was Galarraga who found some redemption with the game-winning hit. After striking out in three previous at-bats, he turned around a Wohlers fastball and sent it into left field for a two-run single, the margin of victory in a Rockies 7-5, 10-inning win.

And who did Baylor send to the mound in the bottom of the 10th to preserve the only playoff victory in franchise history at that point? As late as mid-September, Mark Thompson found himself at Triple-A Colorado Springs, where he helped the Sky Sox win the Pacific Coast League title. He finished the regular season with three solid outings in the Rockies' final series and got a spot on the postseason roster only after an injury sidelined Freeman.

But with Baylor already having blown through five relievers in back of Swift, the choices were Thompson and Reynoso, who never had much success against his former team. Enter Thompson. Three batters later, the young right-hander had his first and only major-league save.

GAME 4

After three nail-biter games decided in the last inning, this one was over early and decisively. Bichette's three-run homer off Maddux in the top of the third vaulted the Rockies into the lead for the fourth consecutive game. But it was short-lived. Castilla's solo homer in the sixth was all the Rockies could add, and a series that featured 11 lead changes and ties ended in a Braves blowout.

Saberhagen's sore shoulder was enough of a pregame question mark that Painter was on call for an emergency start. Saberhagen's constant turning and twisting of his shoulder between pitches signaled trouble, and sure enough, the Braves struck hard in the third, when Jones doubled in two runs before McGriff's homer.

Saberhagen allowed two more runs, and then Game 1 starter Ritz came out of the bullpen and proved ineffective for 1.2 innings. It was 10-4 literally and figuratively for the Rockies' Cinderella season. All they were left with was the moral victory of respect earned from a team that would cruise to a World Series title.

"I'd take Saberhagen in a postseason game anytime," Weiss said. "But he was on fumes before the anthem was done. It was like a boxer going out there and trying to fight with one hand.

"With those two guys (Saberhagen and Swift) healthy, and with our lineup, we would have been the best team in the National League, as far as I'm concerned. At the time, we felt that. But there are no woulda, coulda, shouldas at the professional level. It's all bottom line."

4

BASEBALL WITH AN ALTITUDE

ARENA BASEBALL

Everyone has a favorite baseball-at-altitude memory, the one time when logic disappeared and any sense of normalcy was shattered. In Denver, it occurred so often that baseball was a theatre of the absurd before anybody thought of the humidor.

Gebhard had a feeling things were going to be different because of his days in the Expos organization, which for a time had its Triple-A team in Denver. It didn't take long for his suspicions to be realized: on May 8, 1993, Ruffin took a three-hit shutout into the eighth inning, and the Rockies had built a seemingly safe six-run lead.

"We're playing the Braves at Mile High, and it's late in the game," Gebhard said. "Bases loaded and a left-handed hitter, Sid Bream, breaks his bat and hooks it around the *left*-field foul pole for a grand slam. That was a ball everybody in the park thought was going to be a routine fly-out. That really woke us up as to how the ball carries in the altitude."

First as the hitting coach for three different managers, and then as the man in charge, Hurdle has seen more of the mile-high craziness than anybody.

"The one I remember is when Pedro Astacio reached up to grab Mike Piazza's line drive, and it ended up hitting off the batter's eye beyond the center-field fence," Hurdle recalled. "I couldn't believe it, so we went back and watched the tape.

"Pedro throws the ball to Piazza, outer-third (of the plate) about mid-thigh, Piazza goes out and gets it, and Pedro reaches up like he's going to catch it. And it hits off the center-field batter's eye about halfway up. I've never seen a ball continually climb until it was stopped by a wall. I don't think the ball ever descended."

But Baylor may have said it best when talking about the offensive craziness of baseball at altitude: "When you get in the batter's box, you're in scoring position."

BASEBALL YOU WEREN'T USED TO

Everything you've heard about pre-humidor baseball at Coors Field was true. The ball did travel approximately nine percent farther at mile-high altitude than at sea level. And the dry, thin air did make baseballs slicker and harder to grip, and didn't offer as much resistance for breaking pitches. In short, baseball at 5,280 feet was a hitter's nirvana.

"As far as action of the pitches, there was a difference," Bailey said. "Dante (Bichette) came up with the greatest explanation. He said, 'Give me 10 pitches here and 10 pitches in Atlanta. Out of those 10 in Atlanta, I'm going to see maybe four or five good ones to hit. And of those four or five, maybe two or three I'm going to get a pretty good swing at.

"'Now throw me 10 here, and I'm going to see five, six pitches to hit, and out of those five or six, four or five are going to be pretty good pitches: a flatter slider, a fastball that doesn't move as much, a curveball that hangs.' The chances of something bad happening were greater. There was a significant difference in the way the games were played. Stats don't lie."

It wasn't just the home runs. Many of the tape-measure blasts at Coors Field would fly out of any park. The expansive outfield benefited singles and gap hitters as much as the big boppers. Check out Neifi Perez's career numbers. In six seasons with the Rockies, he was a .282 hitter. In the next six years, he hit higher than .256 only once. He legged out a Rockies club-record 49 triples, but has only had 12 since being traded in 2001.

Neifi Perez, right, won a Gold Glove and still holds the club career record for triples.
AP Images

"It was hard to leave that place," Perez said. "I loved it there."

Added Leskanic: "The park was unforgiving because, first of all, the center fielder plays at about 370 feet, so anything hit in front falls in. I was a part of a couple plays where the ball just got by me on the ground going up the middle, and the hitter ended up with a double because the center fielder was so deep."

For a six-time Gold Glove winner who valued defense as much as offense, Buddy Bell found managing at Coors Field to be filled with new challenges.

"You couldn't react to every big inning," Bell said. "Your pitcher gives up six runs in the first three innings, and you just have to sit there and hope he gets better. Or that the other guy gives up more. It was baseball that I wasn't used to.

"It should be an unbelievably huge home-field advantage, but it isn't because you have to use your bullpen so much. If you have a 10-day homestand, you're screwed. You have to manage a bullpen so much differently than you do anywhere else."

To that end, Baylor would often bring in key relievers in the middle innings to get out of trouble and keep games close, leading the relievers to coin the phrase "Baylor Saves" for those occasions. That jived with Baylor's other Coors Field-only stratagem of playing the infield in to cut off runs early in games.

"I got criticized a lot for playing the infield in early, but I told the guys, 'If we stay within a certain number of runs, we can catch them,'" Baylor said. "When you're down by three, and they have guys on second and third, if you play back and they hit a groundball, now you're down by four. Another groundball, you're down by five. Down three compared to five, it's easier mentally. E.Y. gets on, Kingery bloops one, Dante hits one out. It's tied."

A SWINGING BAT WAS A DANGEROUS BAT

Often times, it wasn't a slugger who performed freakish feats with the bat. Even the little guys had their day, which drove pitchers crazy.

"You were going to give up home runs," Leskanic said. "But I can remember playing against Philadelphia, and that little guy who had about three career homers (Kevin Stocker) hit a couple of bombs against us one day.

"ERAs were soaring at home. And I don't care how much money a guy is making, he's going to look at his ERA. If your ERA is seven-something at home and one-something on the road, after a while it has an effect on you."

The altitude even made Hall of Famers quiver in their spikes.

"I asked Maddux if he would ever pitch here (for the Rockies)," Bailey said. "And he said, 'You couldn't pay me enough. I'm not going to bust my ass for a 4.50 ERA.' Glavine would come into the weight room the next day after pitching and say, 'My body feels like hell. I don't see how you guys do it here.'"

Added Hurdle: "I'd never seen pitchers' confidence levels drop so dramatically as when they were in Coors Field. We'd watch them perform their last two or three starts before coming in here, and they could be rolling. And then they'd come here, and all of a sudden you'd see the hand come to the forehead, they'd be off the mound walking around, the bad body language.

"The highlight of it would be when the elites would come in, and you would actually see them get tested. They would labor. Not just physically but mentally. Every bat that walked up to the plate was a dangerous bat. A swinging bat was a dangerous bat."

Weiss said it was like clockwork. An opposing pitcher could be cruising, but as soon as the Rockies got a couple of runners on base, "It was, 'All right, here we go.' And the pitcher would be visibly shaken out there. The wheels would just come off, and 10 minutes later, we would have seven runs. It was unbelievable. As hitters, we just thrived on that. It was like a shark smelling blood."

Rest assured that Rockies pitchers got more than their fair share of sympathy from opposing hurlers.

"I remember one time against Texas, John Wetteland was closing for them, and he had gotten into multiple games in a series at Coors Field, and had a rough time of it," Dipoto said. "He was in the midst of a great run in his career, but he came over to our bullpen on the third day, looking absolutely defeated, and he said, 'You gotta tell me. How can you guys do this 81 games a year?' And Leskanic looks up and says, 'Well, my friend, we call it a good sense of humor.'"

CHECK THE RECORD BOOK

There are nine pages in the Rockies' media guide devoted entirely to home runs. You name the category, and it's listed.

The longest home run in Coors Field history belongs to an opponent—Piazza at 496 feet on September 26, 1997. You had to hit one at least 482 feet to get into the Coors Field top 10. Twenty-six balls have been hit into the right-field upper deck, with Walker leading the way with eight.

The most home runs hit in a game at Coors Field are 10, happening no fewer than five times. The Rockies have hit as many as six homers in a game three times, and have hit three homers in one inning 22 times.

In fact, the Rockies have three of the top nine single-season home-run totals at home in major-league history: 149 in 1996, 144 in 1999, and 134 in 1995. Coors Field also has three of the top four single-season home run totals: 303 in 1997, 271 in 1996, and 268 in 2001.

Club vice president Jay Alves understands it all now, but when he joined the organization as media relations director in 1998, it took him a while to comprehend.

"We'd pitch back-to-back complete games, and I'd be thinking: that's probably not any kind of record. But it was," Alves said. "Then we'd do something like hit five home runs in a game, and I'm thinking, that must be a record. And I look it up, and it had been done five times already."

DODGING BULLETS

It's all in the numbers. In one memorable four-game series from June 27-30, 1996, the Rockies and Dodgers combined to score 85 runs, hit 25 home runs, and bat .378, with the Rockies at .416.

The final scores were 13-1, 13-4, 13-10, and 16-15. The series finale set a National League record for the longest nine-inning game (four hours and 20 minutes), and in it, the Dodgers hit three consecutive home runs off Thompson, while Young tied a major-league record with six stolen bases.

Yes, these were two teams who didn't like each other, fueled by Baylor's long-standing disdain for everything Dodger Blue, just blasting away at each other over four consecutive days.

"That series with the Dodgers was like two drunks at 2 a.m.," Hurdle said. "One guy would load up a punch, and then the other guy would get up, regain his balance and throw a punch."

SORRY, PAL

The story Swanson likes to tell involves a four-game sweep of the Padres right after the 1996 All-Star break.

"(Then-Padres official) Roger Riley hates it every time I tell it," Swanson said. "They had dominant leads in all four games of the series. In the second game, they had a seven-run lead, Bob Tewksbury was killing us, and then it rained.

"They decided not to bring Tewksbury back after the delay. Vinny (Castilla) hits a grand slam, and we're piecing it back together. Then we went off on their bullpen, scored 11 runs in the seventh inning, and ended up winning the game.

"We did something like that four days in a row. Roger is sitting behind me every day, and keep in mind that he's my best friend in baseball. We were the best men at each other's weddings.

"It gets to Sunday (the last day of the series), and as much as I wanted to win every game we played, I felt bad for him. I didn't know what to say to the guy. Finally, he said, 'Just get me out of this bleepin' place. I've got to get out of here.'"

24-12

Jim Leyland said it with amazement in his voice, eight years after the fact: "One game, we lost 24-12."

This was 1999 pre-humidor Coors Field, where the altitude and the double-figure scores were the diametric opposite of Leyland's little-ball style of offense. That year, the Rockies played 36 home games in which one team scored in double figures. But one game sticks out: Reds 24, Rockies 12 on May 19.

How ridiculous was it? The Rockies had a four-run inning, two three-run innings, and a two-run inning, and still lost by a dozen runs. They had a pitcher allow four earned runs (Roberto Ramirez), five earned runs (Chuck McElroy), six earned runs (Dipoto), and seven earned runs (Brian Bohanon).

The Reds pounded out 28 hits, including six home runs and nine doubles. Jeffrey Hammonds, who would wear a Rockies uniform the following year, had three of those homers and a double, driving in five. Sean Casey hit two homers and drove in six. Six other Reds had at least three hits.

"What I remember is that Rob Butcher, my counterpart with the Reds, kept coming to me with a new record they had set," Alves said. "We kept making announcement after announcement, and they kept setting records."

Chris Haft witnessed the carnage as a visiting beat writer for the *Cincinnati Enquirer.* "I remember writing, 'It was a lot of things, but it wasn't baseball,'" Haft recalled. "Ron Villone came in and pitched three scoreless innings at the end of the game, and that day it was like he was Sandy Koufax."

BALLPARK ALTERATIONS?

Moving in the fences, raising the fences, adding plexiglass and nets on top of the fences—they were all considered as ways to mitigate the offensive damage at pre-humidor Coors Field. But when push came to shove, the park's natural beauty won out, and any potential alterations were scrapped.

"We talked about putting eight to 10 feet of plexiglass on top of the left-field wall to knock down some of those balls," Gebhard said. "But once we had sold all those season tickets in left field, we decided not to do it.

"We also talked about a putting up a screen or net that would have extended from the out-of-town scoreboard (in right field) to in front of the bullpens. But we just never got it done. If I could do it over again, I think I would have pushed a little harder to add that—to not have so many of those cheap home runs into the bullpens."

When O'Dowd replaced Gebhard, the club tracked where every ball was hit in the ballpark for a two-year period.

"We found that a majority of balls shot out in right-center field, and a lot of them got out right down the lines," O'Dowd said. "We looked into coming up the foul line in right field and building a wall that would shrink the rest of the outfield, so you could move your right fielder more into right-center and take away that gap. And we looked into keeping that wall higher all the way around in right-center, in front of the bullpens.

"But the more we thought about it, we decided that once we started going down that path, where would it stop? We decided not to do it because we would be creating a mind-set among our players that we have to change the ballpark to have any chance to win here. Every ballpark has its unique qualities, and that's ours."

BUT AT WHAT COST?

For all the offensive fireworks—batting titles, home-run crowns, All-Star berths, even a National League MVP—the fact remains that the best the Rockies ever did in a pre-humidor full season was 83 wins.

The main problem was that things were slanted so far to the offensive side that building a pitching staff that could be successful over a stretch of years was impossible. The 1995 team reached the playoffs relying far too heavily on its bullpen, but that proved to be a one-year aberration.

Switching to entirely different conditions on the road also proved too difficult a task to overcome. In fact, nobody associated with the franchise believes that winning was sustainable over a long period of time at pre-humidor Coors Field.

"When you look at all the offensive talent this club had back in 1995-1998, and think about the fact that the most wins they ever had was 83, you really have to ask the question, how could that happen?" O'Dowd said. "How could you not at least average 86 wins and be 10 games over .500 a year?

"You couldn't build a team the same way as you would in St. Louis, San Francisco, San Diego. And you know what? Until the humidor came along, I'm not sure there was a formula. Not long-term."

Hurdle said it would have taken a bunch of pitchers to have their careers take off at the same time: "You can't go out and buy them. We tried that. We sent a lot of guys to the All-Star Game every year, and offensively, they did some great things. But all said and done, we weren't playing in October."

Added Siegle: "My heart said that, sure, if you have the talent, you should be able to win in Coors Field regardless of the conditions. But my head said it was impossible because you couldn't keep a stable pitching staff. No, you really couldn't win there. Not consistently."

5

THE BLAKE STREET BOMBERS

BOMBS AWAY

"They had a name for them," Hurdle said. "You don't give people names unless there is some significance to it."

They were the Blake Street Bombers, and they lived up to that name in a way that altered record books and scared the daylights out of opposing pitchers. Galarraga and Bichette were the originals. Burks came along a year later. Walker arrived in 1995, when Castilla rose from backup infielder to true Bomber. A few years later, Helton got in on the act.

Their numbers and accomplishments were mind-boggling, even in an era when bulked up sluggers smashed records and raised power-hitting standards to levels the game hadn't seen before: Bichette won the home run and RBI title in 1995. Galarraga won back-to-back RBI titles in 1996 and 1997, and the home run title in 1996. Walker made it three Rockies in a row winning the home run title in 1997. Burks had a year for the ages in 1996. Four Bombers hit at least 30 homers in 1996, '97, and '98. Three hit 40 or more in two of those years.

And they were so much more than just power hitters. Galarraga won the batting title in 1993 with a .370 mark. Walker won three in four years at .363, .379, and .372, with Helton taking the other at .372. No wonder the running joke was that Hurdle, who served as the hitting instructor through the latter half of the Bombers' destructive years, had the easiest job in sports.

"I was fortunate enough to enter into an opportunity where we had four guys whose careers popped while they were playing at Coors Field—Walker, Bichette, Galarraga, and Castilla," Hurdle said. "And Burks was on the periphery. It was an experience I'll never forget.

"I had played on good teams, and watched good players play. But I'd never watched four guys do the things offensively that those four did. They were dynamic. It was special. For this organization, that's always going to be a special time. This whole city embraced it.

"To put it in proper perspective: to go out on the market—and every winter it escalates—and get four players in their prime who play corner positions, it could be anywhere from $40 to $80 million now. Just for those four guys."

No, you couldn't do it now unless you had a Yankee-like payroll. But Gebhard did it. Castilla was picked in the second round of the expansion draft. Galarraga took a bargain-basement salary of $500,000 to continue working with Baylor, who helped him turn things around in St. Louis in 1992. Bichette came in arguably the best deal in Rockies history, made on expansion-draft day. Burks also came relatively cheaply as a free agent. Only Walker was a big-ticket item on the market.

All of them in pre-humidor Coors Field at the same time . . . yes, it was the perfect storm of slugging.

"A number of factors came into play," Hurdle said. "Any time you have an expansion, the liquidation of the pitching suffers to some degree. But also, these guys popped. Their confidence was never higher. The park was hitter-friendly. Don's style was a great fit for the ballpark. From an offensive standpoint, that was as good as it gets. I just didn't want to screw it up. You don't want to be the guy spinning the plates who lets the one plate fall off."

No, nothing could mess up the Blake Street Bombers—still the most memorable figures in franchise history.

THE FIVE-TOOL CANADIAN

Sixteen years into their existence, the Rockies still don't have a Hall of Famer. The only Cooperstown inductee with any connection to the franchise sits in the press box, wears cowboy hats, and didn't play organized baseball beyond Babe Ruth League. That would be *Rocky Mountain News* baseball writer Tracy Ringolsby, whose three-plus decades chronicling the game got him elected by the Baseball Writers Association of America in 2006.

The only Rockies player who garnered any legitimate support is Dale Murphy, and he spent all of six weeks with the club at the beginning of the 1993 season, far removed from his salad days as a two-time National League MVP.

The late Darryl Kile got seven votes in his only year on the ballot in 2003—the same amount Saberhagen received in 2007. Bichette got three votes in his only ballot appearance in 2007. Weiss got a lone vote in 2006.

Walker's initial appearance will come in 2011, and while there is legitimate doubt about whether he will collect enough votes, there is no arguing the fact that he is the most-talented player to ever wear a Rockies uniform.

"Larry is the most gifted player I've ever come across," Hurdle said. "I played with George Brett, so from my standpoint, this is a very significant comment. The way it turned out, was George a better all-around ballplayer? That's probably an argument. But he was not more gifted."

Siegle has 43 years of front-office experience in the game, including stints with teams that included Hall of Famers Joe Morgan, Mike Schmidt, and Barry Bonds. He says: "Tool for tool, Larry Walker is arguably, if not the best player I've been around, then at least the top three.

"I think Walker was a better player than Bonds. Bonds is a great, great hitter, but he wasn't a particularly good outfielder later in his career. Larry was the type of player who was worth the price of admission just to watch him play."

Bailey was Walker's teammate for a couple of seasons, and has remained around the Major Leagues working in the Rockies' front office, and as a broadcaster. He concurs with Siegle.

"Larry Walker is the best player I have ever seen, played with, played against, whatever," Bailey said. "He can run circles around Barry Bonds. I don't care what anybody else ever says. Is Barry Bonds a great hitter? Yes. He's the greatest hitter I've ever seen. But he's not the complete player Larry Walker was. I'll carry that to my grave. Larry Walker could do things that were amazing."

Bichette agreed: "Walker is the most talented player I ever played with, and I played with Paul Molitor, Robin Yount, and Ken Griffey Jr. Larry did everything well. I remember a stretch during the year he won the MVP. He was locked in. He was hitting the ball so hard, it looked like he was playing golf. It was like he was using his driver every at-bat. Every ball he hit was a screaming line drive. There was a different sound when he hit it."

Dipoto is as much a baseball historian as a reliever turned front office executive. His opinion: "I don't know if Larry will get in the Hall of Fame, but he should. I didn't get to see Mickey Mantle play, but I can't imagine it was much different. I mean, what was Mantle going to do any better? Switch-hit, that's about it. Larry was that good. I would have paid money just to see him play defense.

"I said to him one day, 'Dude, you're one of the 10 best players I've ever seen in my life.'

"And he said, 'C'mon.'

"And I said, 'No really. You do things I've never seen anybody else do.'

"And he said, 'How about top 500 at best?'

"And then he walked away. He was a very humble guy for somebody with all that talent."

RAW TALENT, RARE MIND

Walker was a hockey player at heart. He played little baseball as a youth in Maple Ridge, British Columbia, and turned to the game full-time only after his career as a goalie hit a dead end at hockey's Junior A level.

As the oft-told story goes, he was so raw and inexperienced as a

Rookie Ball player in the Expos organization that one day, when he had to retreat to first base after a fly ball was caught in the gap, he cut directly across the diamond, not knowing he had to retouch second base. Then he argued with the umpire who called him out.

From that, he grew into a .313 lifetime hitter, a National League MVP, three-time batting champion, and seven-time Gold Glove winner. He hit .350 or higher four times in a five-year span, peaking at .379 in 1999. His 1997 MVP year was one of the best ever posted in any era: .366 batting average, 49 home runs, 130 RBIs, 33 stolen bases, and 143 runs scored.

"Larry might be the only player I've ever run across who I watched develop baseball instincts," Hurdle said. "More often than not, you either have baseball instincts, or you don't. Instincts aren't easily taught, and I'm not sure we taught him instincts. I think he figured it all out. He was borderline genius in those areas. When it came to picking up certain things, the nuances of the game, pitchers—he was amazing."

Added Baylor: "You talk about five tools, but he had the sixth one. He had instincts—when to bunt, when to steal, when to take the extra base. He's the best I have managed."

BATTING CAGE LEGEND

Nobody spent more time watching and working with Walker than Hurdle, not that Walker needed much coaching.

"My first year (as the hitting instructor), I remember saying to Larry, 'Hey, I'm just going to watch you, learn your swing, keep an eye on things, and if I have anything to add, I will.' And he says, 'Yeah, whatever.' I watch April, I watch May, I watch June. It wasn't until the first week of August that I said, 'You want to go down to the cage early and try something?'

"And he was great when we'd go down there because he pretty much knew what he had to tighten up. And the way he went about it . . . he'd say, 'What do you want to do, Coach? What do you want to work on, Coach?' He always called me Coach. And it became more of a game

than a work session. There was always a big kid in there who wanted to have fun.

"Some days I'd get in the chair (behind the pitching machine), and he would stand there and look around. And then he would point somewhere and say, 'OK, I'm going to try to hit the ball there so it will carom off the wall and hit you.'

"And I'd feed it, and wherever it would go, he could hit it so it would deflect right at me. His hand/eye coordination and the way he could handle a bat were as good as I've ever come across."

THE DEKE

And then there was Walker's patented deke play. If you've seen it, you know what a thing of beauty it was:

A ball was hit over Walker's head, but instead of turning his back to the infield and running it down, he made it appear to the base-runner that he was going to catch it. The base-runner froze, or at least slowed down, the ball went over Walker's head, he quickly retrieved the carom off the wall, and managed to limit the runner's advancement by a base or two.

"I had a teammate in Kansas City, Tom Poquette, who did that play, but I haven't seen anybody else do it," Hurdle said. "And nobody did it as well or as often as Larry. Even after he went to St. Louis and we told our guys about it, he did it against us, and one of our guys bit on it. It was just fantastic."

Baylor remembers another one during the first week of the 1995 season, the first in Coors Field.

"We're playing Cincinnati, and Walk doesn't know that wall out there," Baylor said. "I think (Barry) Larkin hit a ball at him, and he does this (simulating pounding a mitt, as if about to catch the ball), then turns around, plays the ball off the wall, and just throws a BB to second base, holding the guy to a single. I said, 'You've got to be kidding me.'"

It's unanimous—Larry Walker is the most talented player to have worn a Rockies uniform. *AP Images*

SOMETHING ABOUT THE NUMBER THREE

Throughout his career, Walker was obsessively superstitious about the number three. Of course, he wore number 33, but that was only the beginning.

"My first marriage occurred at 3:33 p.m. on November the third," Walker said. "When I was in Montreal, the last two years I donated 33 tickets in section 333 at Olympic Stadium. When I set the alarm clock, the minutes are always set at 33.

"Before getting into the batter's box, I always took three practice swings. If it didn't feel right, I'd take three more, not one. But I'm superstitious about my superstitions. If I let too many of them out of the bag, they might not work for me anymore. So I don't share them with too many people."

But teammates knew about them anyway.

"When I saw him put something in the microwave, he put it on 33 minutes and 33 seconds," Leskanic said. "And the whole shower room will be empty except for one guy using the third one, and he'll wait until that person gets out."

Multiples of three were OK, too. Walker's pregame routine included listening to six heavy metal songs, one always being Motley Crue's "Angela," his wife's name. Three others were by the group Skid Row: "Eighteen and Life," "I Remember," and "Quicksand Jesus." The other two changed daily.

TOO LITTLE OR TOO MUCH?

Walker's major-league career stretched 17 seasons—from 20 games as a 22-year-old rookie with the Expos in 1989 to 100 games as a 38-year-old veteran with the St. Louis Cardinals in 2005. In all, he appeared in 1,988 games and accumulated 6,907 at-bats.

But if you add up all the time he spent on the disabled list due to various injuries, he lost almost four complete seasons. That will definitely hurt his chances at the Hall of Fame, as will the anti-Coors Field bias voters have against Rockies hitters.

There were also some questions about his lack of desire to play on occasion, especially late in the seasons when the Rockies weren't contending, which was most years. Let the debate rage:

"There was a knock on Larry for not playing hurt," Bell said. "But what happened was, he played a lot more than he should have, and eliminated a couple of years he could have kept playing. He was so big, but he played like he was five-foot-four, and he beat up his body.

"It used to piss me off, the battles I had with coaches and other people in the organization about Larry's presence, or what his affect on our team was. For me, it was always positive. You know what? Larry Walker has no interest in playing for something that doesn't mean anything. I understood that. He was great for me in the clubhouse. He was a good teammate to the guys who really cared."

Added Dipoto: "I don't think anybody realized how badly Larry wanted to win. But in reality, what drives a guy? I don't think Larry cared about how much money he made. I know he didn't care about his numbers. A lot of the criticism was that he shuts it down—you can't count on him. When he's not winning, I think he would get a little bored with it."

Siegle's take: "Larry had every possible tool to put him in the Hall of Fame. Unfortunately, he didn't take care of himself as well as he could have. But he was one of the best I've been around, and I've been around a lot of Hall of Famers. I don't know if Larry will ever be a Hall of Famer, but he had the ability to be.

"He played 15-16 years, but if you boil it down, it might come out to about 10 or 11. But what a player he was. He had the capability to have years like that MVP year of his, every single year. But I don't think he worked real hard keeping himself in shape."

SLEDGEHAMMER—A STEAL OF A DEAL

Ask Gebhard to name the best trade he made in his eight-year stay with the Rockies, and he is quick to answer. It was his first, back on expansion-draft day. The swap, Bichette for Reimer, wasn't announced until after the draft, but it was actually agreed upon earlier that morning.

"I had been talking to Sal Bando of Milwaukee," Gebhard recalled. "Dante wasn't going to be a regular there, so we tried to find a way to work out a deal. I was afraid that if Dante was left out there in the draft, Florida might take him, because he grew up down there.

"Sal was looking for a left-handed designated hitter, and I saw him in the lobby that morning, and I said, 'Kevin Reimer.' And he said, 'Yeah.' So we drafted Reimer off Texas' roster, and traded him for Dante. And I'd say that one turned out pretty well."

Reimer, a lumbering left-handed power hitter, batted .249 with 13 homers and 60 RBIs in 437 at-bats for Milwaukee in 1993, and never played in the Major Leagues again.

As for Bichette, in the Rockies' record book, he is third all-time in RBIs, hits, runs, doubles, extra-base hits, total bases, and stolen bases, fourth in games played, at-bats, and home runs, and fifth in batting average and slugging percentage. As if that wasn't enough, he was one of the most popular Rockies. Not bad for a guy who before that expansion-draft day trade thought about taking his career to Japan.

"When I was with Milwaukee in 1992, Sal Bando saw me bumming one day, and he came up and talked to me," Bichette said. "He said I had the most power on the team, the best arm, and that I was a good two-strike hitter.

"And I said, 'Exactly. You think that about me, but I'm still not playing every day.' He promised me that if I wasn't going to play every day (in Milwaukee), he would get me a chance somewhere else. He was a pretty fair guy.

"I remember during that first spring training with the Rockies, Jerry McMorris was talking to the team, telling us it was the opportunity of a lifetime for a lot of guys. I took it personally. I was thinking: he's talking to me, man, because I was not a rookie. I was 29. I knew I had to get it done, or I might not get another chance."

GROOVE-Y KIND OF FEELING

Their relationship began in Milwaukee—hitting instructor and pupil. Their subsequent moves to Colorado put Baylor in the position

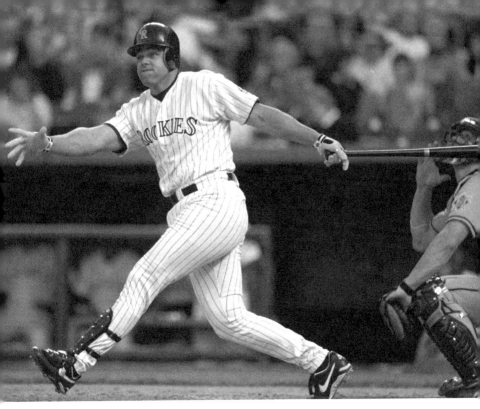

Dante Bichette was regarded as goofy, but he was all business with a bat in his hands.
AP Images

of being Bichette's ultimate boss. But there was always a worried father/wayward son relationship underneath it all.

"Dante was unique; an individual," Baylor said with a smile. "We battled. We locked horns. He kind of thought like a left-hander sometimes. I'd talk him out of things. I'd talk to him about being on time. We'd go round and round with that. I knew I could get on him in a way that he knew I was right.

"In Milwaukee, he had me keep a chart of how many bad pitches he swung at. I'd do that for two weeks, and I'd say, 'I'm tired. I'm filling this book up.' But he felt like he could hit any pitch thrown by anybody. And with two strikes, he was one of the better hitters. Who did you want up with the game on the line? You wanted Dante. He loved it. He'd always take that challenge on."

Bichette recalled that Baylor knew exactly what buttons to push with him.

"A couple of months into that first season (1993), I'm hitting around .260, Don came to me. He told me to stop thinking so much, and to be more aggressive. He said I was trying too hard, trying to be perfect, and that I just needed to see the first good pitch to hit, and go after it. Let the ability come out. I got three or four hits that night against Houston, and got hot after that. That's when it turned around for me.

"He always knew what I was thinking, or what I needed to do. I played for a lot of managers, but I consider him the best. He really knew his players. He was in tune with them. He knew the offensive player."

MATCHMAKER, MATCHMAKER

Baylor also played a key role in the most important development in Bichette's personal life—his marriage to Marianna.

"We're out hitting early one day in Fenway Park in 1991, and Dante comes over to me and says, 'I just met a girl I think I could marry,'" Baylor said.

"I said, 'What's her name?'"

"And he said, 'I don't know.'"

"I said, 'What do you mean, you don't know?'"

"And he said, 'Well, she works over in the health club behind the Green Monster.'"

"So it's about 2:30, 3:00, and I said, 'You better finish hitting, shower, go back over there, and introduce yourself.' So he went back over there, invited her to a game, and they're still married today. She was quite an influence on him. She made him realize that baseball was important."

IF THE SONG FITS . . .

Signature songs are as much a part of the game today as setup relievers. A player comes to the plate, or a closer runs in from the bullpen, and you hear his personal anthem blare.

Trevor Hoffman and AC/DC's "Hells Bells" are legendary in San

Diego. The Ozzy Osbourne song "Crazy Train" has belonged to both Walker and Chipper Jones. But no player and song were any better fit than Bichette and Peter Gabriel's "Sledgehammer."

First of all, Bichette had the biceps to swing a sledgehammer. In fact, in between the 1993 and 1994 seasons, Bichette and teammate Chris Jones won the Pro Baseball Players Arm Wrestling championship in Las Vegas, with Bichette going unbeaten in the event.

Hurdle loves to talk about a particular Bichette feat of strength: "Every once in a while, he'd get the bat in one hand and swing it, and he would hit balls out of the park off me in batting practice, swinging one-handed. I've never seen anybody else do that."

Truth be told, "Sledgehammer" first belonged to Dave Parker, the man for whom Bichette was traded in 1992, when he went from the Angels to the Brewers.

"That was his song, and if you remember, he used to swing a sledgehammer in the on-deck circle," Bichette said. "I thought it was kind of cool. I stole it from him."

Bichette said his weight training began early in his career, when he was in the Angels organization.

"The Angels were one of the first teams to get into the weight room," he said. "Our hitting instructor, Rick Down, was a body builder, a big guy. It started for me there. I kept at it throughout my career, and really didn't perfect my workout routine until late in it, after I left the Rockies."

Bichette's constantly varying body weights, training regimens, and results also made for a constant source of clubhouse jokes.

"It was almost comical," Dipoto said. "One year, he would show up looking like Hulk Hogan, then the next year, Jack LaLanne."

SERIOUS BUSINESS

The T-shirt was a classic: "Bichette Happens" is what it said—two words that perfectly captured all things Dante: the offensive firepower, the defensive lapses, the beat-of-his-own-drummer behavior.

But when it came to hitting, there was nothing goofy about

Bichette's approach. He was a student of that aspect of the game, and never stopped tinkering, adjusting, and working to get the most out of his ability. Hurdle saw this first-hand as Bichette's hitting coach through much of his stay with the Rockies.

"He was as intelligent a hitter as I've run across," Hurdle said. "He knew his swing, he knew what he wanted to do. He knew how he needed to do it. They said he was goofy, but not when it came to hitting. That was his passion. He was able to follow his passion.

"What I remember most about Dante was his ability to drive in a run on a pitcher's pitch at a dramatic time in the game. He wasn't a cripple hitter by any stretch of the imagination. He could hit good pitches in good locations—pitchers' pitches—and late in games."

Bichette's take shows there was a deep thinker behind that laid-back demeanor.

"I got the 'goofy' label early on," he said. "I don't know if it was the long hair, or what. I've tried to analyze it over the years. That laid-back attitude I had was, I believe, a reason why I hit so well late in games and in pressure situations. I was relaxed, not so worried. But maybe that kept me from applying myself defensively, or getting more out of my ability. So it had its pros and cons."

TRIVIAL PURSUITS

Bichette's studious side wasn't limited to just hitting. He was also a student of the game's history. And he loved a challenge.

"Every day for the years I was with the Rockies, I gave Dante a trivia quiz," Dipoto said. "I started by giving him layups, but later on, I was throwing some tough ones at him.

"One day, he came over to the bullpen during a game in 1998 and he said, 'I got you. I got you.'

"And I said, 'What have you got?'

"And he said, 'Tell me who is the only player in history to go 40-40; 40 homers and 40 outfield assists.'

"I said, 'It's never been done. I'm not buying it.'

"And he says, 'Yes it has. Think about it.'

"So every day, I'm coming up with guys. I'm guessing. He would not tell me. All year long, I was too proud to go look it up. So at the end of the year, Dante gave me a bat that I put in my collection, and he wrote out the trivia question on one side of the bat. Then he flipped it over and wrote the answer on the other side: Chuck Klein.

"I went back and looked, and he was right. I never would have believed that would be possible. But after finding out who it was, I knew enough about the history of the game to know that Chuck Klein played in the Baker Bowl, where there was a wall 275 feet away in right field, and people were hitting them off the wall, and he was throwing them out at second base.

"I asked Dante, 'Where did you get that one from?'

"And he said, 'When I came up with the Angels, my first 10 days or so in the big leagues, I hit five home runs and had five outfield assists. And our TV guys said, 'He may be the first guy since Chuck Klein to hit 40 homers and have 40 outfield assists.' That's the only way I knew it.'"

THE MVP THAT WASN'T

Bichette's memorable Opening-Day walkoff blast was just the beginning of a brilliant 1995 season. He would go on to win two of three Triple Crown categories with 40 homers and 128 RBIs, and his .340 batting average was third behind Tony Gwynn. He also led the league in total bases, extra-base hits, and slugging percentage.

But where Bichette didn't finish first was in the Most Valuable Player Award. Larkin, who led Cincinnati to a division title by hitting .319 with 98 runs scored, 51 steals, but only 15 homers and 66 RBIs, picked up 11 first-place votes and totaled 281 points.

Bichette got six first-place votes—one fewer than third-place finisher Greg Maddux—and finished with 251 points. The vote was as much an indictment of Coors Field's inflationary effect on offensive numbers as anything. And it certainly didn't help that Bichette had a streak of 17 consecutive home runs there. Still, the results leave Bichette miffed to this day.

"Looking back at it now, I could have acted a little more frustrated,"

Bichette said. "I decided not to. It's obvious that it was a little bit of an injustice. The Coors Field thing got me. They just weren't going to give it to me. But when you look at it, I had a big second half—27 home runs, a ton of RBIs. Barry (Larkin) had a nice year. But that was a tough one to accept. It's definitely the one that got away. I'd say that was the most frustrating point in my career."

Baylor agreed with his slugger.

"No doubt about it," he said. "He should have won it."

FROM THE OUTHOUSE . . .

Welcome to Galarraga's 1992 nightmare:

Acquired by the St. Louis Cardinals the previous winter for popular right-hander Ken Hill, Galarraga lasted all of two games and seven at-bats into the season before a Wally Whitehurst pitch broke a bone in his hand.

Forty games later, Galarraga returned and began a prolonged offensive struggle that broke his spirit and almost got him released. As Galarraga's strikeouts kept piling up and his batting average bottomed out below .200, Torre had no other alternative. One game, he pinch-hit for his struggling first baseman.

His confidence shattered, Galarraga went back to the clubhouse, and Baylor, his hitting instructor at the time, followed. And it was then that Baylor began to work a miracle that would benefit his future employers in Colorado.

"Cat had never been pinch-hit for," Baylor said. "So I went into the locker room with him, trying to console him. He was trying to drink some water in a cup, and his hands were just quivering. He couldn't keep any water in the glass. He was so upset.

"I told him, 'This is what I see. They're jamming you like crazy. Are you willing to make the commitment? We have to change."

"He said, 'I'll do whatever.'

"I said, 'You can't listen to your wife, your agent, your attorney. It's got to be the two of us. I don't know if it's going to work, but we have to try something.' If he was going to change anything, this was the time, when he was at the bottom. He was hanging on by a thread. And that's when I opened up his stance, changed his swing completely.

"I knew one thing for sure, he wasn't seeing the baseball in that closed position. I turned him open to get a better look, and bam, it just hit him. We always talk about a dominant eye, and he was right-eye dominant. When his stance was closed, he was looking with his left eye.

"This opened up a whole new world for him. He had a good second half from there. He started seeing the breaking ball again, hitting the fastball again. He hit a long home run in Chicago near the end of the year, and he was thrilled. He was like a kid again."

. . . TO THE CATBIRD SEAT

For all the man hours logged by Gebhard and his staff of scouts in the months leading up to the expansion draft, one of the pillars of the franchise's early days fell right into their laps.

Even after Baylor helped Galarraga save his career with the new stance, the Cardinals weren't interested in bringing him back in 1993. So Galarraga needed a place to play, and naturally he turned to Baylor's new team.

"The agent called and said, 'You can afford him. We'll make the money right,'" Gebhard said. "I remember calling Don and saying, 'We can sign Galarraga. All he wants is a half-million dollars. Do you think he can still hit?' And Don said, 'Yeah, I think he can.'"

And just like that, the Rockies had a cleanup hitter, Gold Glove-caliber first baseman, clubhouse leader, and fan favorite. But not even Baylor, the man who saved Galarraga's career, could have envisioned what followed: A batting title in 1993, a home-run title in 1996, and RBI titles in 1996 and 1997—a Blake Street Bomber by any measure.

"Cat's career turned around, thanks to Don, and to getting healthy," Gebhard said.

A HARD .370

For a nine-year period beginning in 1993, the National League batting title was the exclusive property of the Rockies and Gwynn.

Nobody else could crack the fraternity; Galarraga started the streak in 1993, followed by four titles in a row from Gwynn. Then Walker won two in a row, Todd Helton got his first, followed by another from Walker.

But none of those were more unexpected than Galarraga's, especially considering that his .370 title-winning average was 127 points higher than his average the previous season in St. Louis.

"And it was a hard .370," Baylor said.

The only question was: would Galarraga accumulate enough plate appearances to qualify for the title after twice spending time on the disabled list that season? But he finished with a flourish and was named the National League's player of the month that September.

"The next year, when the Louisville Slugger people showed up to present him the (Silver) bat, he wanted me to go out there with him for the presentation," Baylor said. "He said to me, 'You're responsible, and I want you to go out there with me.'

"I said, 'Nope, you did it, you go out there and take your bows.'

"But that was special to me that he wanted me to go out there with him. As long as he knew we worked together to get it done, that's all I needed."

THERE'S NO WAY

You'd think the longest, most majestic and awe-inspiring home run in Rockies history would have happened in Denver, right? How could it not, with the distance-adding effects of baseball played at 5,280 feet?

But while there have been many memorable blasts of nearly 500 feet at Coors Field, it was Galarraga's homer in what was then Pro Player Stadium in Florida on May 31, 1997, that still has those who saw it shaking their heads in amazement.

This was a grand slam in more ways than one. Yes, the blast scored four runs to give the Rockies a 7-0 lead in the fourth inning off one of their nemeses, Kevin Brown. And the official measurement according

Andres Galarraga won a batting title, a home-run title, and two RBI crowns in a Rockies uniform. *AP Images*

to the Marlins' media guide was 529 feet, still the longest in stadium history. But that doesn't tell the whole story.

"Very rarely do men get goose bumps, and when Cat hit the ball off Kevin Brown in Florida, I had goose bumps," said Hurdle, who was coaching first base at the time. "I watched that spot. I went back to the dugout. I keep a book. I marked down the section and the row.

"Later that winter, my wife, Carla, and I went to a football game there, and I asked for tickets in that specific spot, and we watched a football game from that spot. And there's no way. *No way.* There's people sitting around me, and I want to tell them, but they wouldn't understand. I don't know how many times I told Carla, 'There's no way.'

"The funny thing is, initially, 590-something feet came up (on the scoreboard) and it was up for just a flash, and then it went off. Somebody said to wait a minute, and they changed it. Ten seconds later, 520-something came up, and they kept it up there.

"That is the farthest ball I've ever seen hit, anywhere. (Mark) McGwire hit a ball during batting practice that ended up in the players' parking lot (at Coors Field)—that's about the only one I can compare to Cat's. The only way you can really experience it is to go sit in that seat. It was section 413, about 11 rows up."

A PRO'S PRO

Yes, Galarraga was a big, strong man. The media guide listed him at 6-foot-3 and 235 pounds, but he was probably more like 250-260. Everything about him was big—legs, arms, barrel chest.

"Cat was so physically intimidating," Hurdle said. "And I don't think I ever saw him in the weight room. When you would throw batting practice to him, he would hit balls that had a different sound than anybody else's. When Cat would square it up, it almost sounded as if it were coming out of a gun."

But Galarraga's nickname, Big Cat, fit him to a "T", because for a man so large, he was nimble and graceful around the first-base bag.

"You looked at him, and you wouldn't think he could move at all," Siegle said. "But he was a brilliant defensive first baseman who made the left side of the infield even better by being able to make unbelievable catches at first base on throws.

"One that stands out: we were playing St. Louis, and we were winning in the bottom of the ninth. They had two outs and two on, and somebody hit a screamer down the third base line that Vinny made a miraculous stab on, then threw it, and Andres made an unbelievable stretch to catch it and end the game. It was one of the most memorable plays on both ends that I've ever seen."

It's no coincidence that Galarraga was Castilla's mentor and role model.

"When I came here in 1993, my English wasn't very good," Castilla said. "Cat took care of me, man. On the road, we'd eat together every day and always go to the ballpark together.

"He didn't talk much about leadership. He led by example. He was always ready to play. He played hurt. He was popular. Everybody liked him. When you saw him, he always had a big smile. I followed what he did.

"He would get you to take infield. Sometimes, you wouldn't feel like doing it, but he'd say, 'C'mon man, it's showtime. Let's go.' He was an All-Star. If he would take infield, you had to do it too."

THE BITTER END

But all good things come to an end, and Gebhard remembers that in this case, it came much too quickly for his liking. Galarraga left in a rush after the 1997 season to sign a three-year, $25-million deal with the Atlanta Braves.

"I tried to negotiate all summer with him and the agent, and they didn't want to talk about it," Gebhard said. "Then we got to the off-season, and I got a call one morning from the agent, and he said, 'I'm ready to talk about Andres. I have an offer from a National League club, and they want an answer by sundown.' After trying to talk to him for five months, they gave us five hours.

"They didn't want to talk about anything less than three times eight—$24 million over three years. I was very nervous about going more than two years. We had a guy at Triple-A who was just about ready,

Mr. Helton, and Don (Baylor) was nervous about giving Andres three years, too. We made an offer of two years and an option that with incentives would have been about $24 million. But it wasn't guaranteed. They called back at 5 p.m. and said, 'We're going to Atlanta.'"

It was a sad and shocking departure, the first of the Bombers to go.

"That was the only time that I ever exposed the numbers in a contract negotiation," Gebhard said. "But this one I had to say because the people, the fans, the media, needed to know what happened.

"Andres had a good first year in Atlanta, then he sat out the second year with cancer, then he came back and played the third year. So, we didn't make a bad decision. Besides, Helton came in and held his own. He turned out OK."

COUSIN VINNY—A PLEASANT SURPRISE

Gebhard criss-crossed the country in the months leading up to the expansion draft, but one team he made sure to see a lot of was the Braves. And why not? They were just beginning an amazing run of consecutive division titles, and were loaded with talent that couldn't fit onto their protected list. But Gebhard didn't think he had a chance at Castilla, mostly because Cox told him as much.

"I remember watching spring training one day, and they had a shortstop out there taking infield," Gebhard said. "And Bobby Cox came over and said, 'Don't even think about that guy, because he won't be available.' It was Vinny.

"But they got caught up in numbers. They had so many good players that Vinny was left unprotected. We thought we were getting a shortstop who didn't have much range, but we liked his bat. We thought, well, he and Freddy Benavides could battle it out, and we found out which one was better, didn't we?"

In Rockies history, Castilla is second in at-bats, third in home runs and games played, and fourth in hits, runs, RBIs, doubles, extra-base hits, and total bases.

"That (expansion draft) was the best thing that happened to me," Castilla said. "I was playing shortstop at Triple-A, and they had Jeff

Blauser in the big leagues, and Chipper Jones was behind me at Double-A. It would have been very tough for them to protect me."

THIRD WAS THE CHARM

Baylor knew he had something special in his part-time shortstop one day in Mile High Stadium back in 1993.

"I put on a hit-and-run, and I found out about Vinny's power," Baylor said. "He hit one off the top of the wall in right-center. You could see the bat, but I said, 'OK, where am I going to play him?'"

That season, Castilla was part of a shortstop platoon with the light-hitting, slick-fielding Benavides. But the Rockies signed Weiss to be their everyday shortstop in 1994, turning Castilla into a utility infielder.

Ultimately, the answer came during the strike that shortened both the 1994 and 1995 seasons. The Rockies had tired of Hayes' high-maintenance act, and didn't want to re-sign him at $3-million-plus per season for 1995 and beyond. So Gebhard hatched another plan.

"Bob Gebhard called me during the strike and asked me if I wanted to go to the instructional league and learn how to play third base," Castilla said. "I said, 'Sure.' Gene Glynn worked with me down there, and he really helped me a lot. I owe him a lot.

"After the instructional league, I went to winter ball, and I started to hit some home runs. In the minors, I was skinny. I was hitting 15 homers a year. But I started getting bigger around that time."

And right from the beginning, it was clear that Castilla at third base was the perfect example of talent running into opportunity. In his first season as an everyday third baseman, Castilla finished with 32 homers and 90 RBIs, and unexpectedly wound up starting in the All-Star Game, since Giants third baseman Matt Williams was injured. Denver's "Cousin Vinny" was on his way to become his native Mexico's version of Babe Ruth.

FUNNY IN TWO LANGUAGES

Castilla's popularity cut across racial lines in and out of the clubhouse. The reason was simple: he always had a smile on his face

and something funny to say. After he called you "Cuz," of course. He called everybody "Cuz."

"Everybody thought it was because of the movie *My Cousin Vinny*," Castilla said. "But that wasn't it. In Mexico, it was "Bato." You'd say, 'What's up, Bato?' One day, somebody said to me, 'What's up, Cuz?' And it just stuck in my head. I started calling everybody that."

Dipoto was Castilla's teammate for three seasons, and says, "Vinny was funny in two languages. We all used to hang out in the sauna after games. It was like a refuge. Vinny would come in there every night. One time, he's leaning on his knees, and he's shaving. He had just had a magnificent game, this was in 1998, when he had as good a year as you possibly could have.

"He looked up and said to me, 'Cuz, I got the total package, don't I?'

"I said, 'What are you talking about?'

"And he said, 'I got the *bat*. I got the *power*. I got the *leather*.'

"And everybody in the room was howling. The ordinary guy says that, and you don't find it funny. But the way Vinny says it, you're dying, because it's Vinny. He had an unbelievable sense of humor."

Hurdle thinks Castilla's pleasant disposition was part of his success as a hitter.

"For me, one of Vinny's best strengths was that he had no remembrance of yesterday," Hurdle said. "It didn't matter if he was 4-for-4 or 0-for-4 with three punchouts. He showed up the same way the next day. Him and Cat . . . you couldn't tell what happened yesterday when they showed up at the park.

"And with Vinny, it was great because if he was 0-for-20, he didn't know it was 0-for-20. Or if he did, he never let on. He'd just go, 'Hey, Cuz. Today's the day. I'm gonna rake somebody today. I'm gonna get some cheese.'

"He had all these sayings. He worked so hard on his English that he

---

Vinny Castilla remains the best position player to emerge from his native Mexico.
AP Images

became a master of the English language and clichés—and with his accent, he would just make you laugh."

NATIVE SON

Castilla's career numbers are impressive by any measure: a .276 career batting average, 320 home runs, and 1,105 RBIs. Only two third basemen in history have more consecutive 30-plus homer seasons than Castilla's five in a row, 1995-99. Only seven third basemen have hit more home runs. But when it comes to position players from Mexico, there is no comparison. Castilla is the best—ever.

And in a pomp-and-circumstance day befitting Elvis or Michael Jordan, Castilla got a chance to start the 1999 regular season with a game in Monterrey, Mexico, between the Rockies and Padres—the first time a major-league season began off American soil.

It was Easter Sunday, April 4, and the streets of Monterrey buzzed with excitement and anticipation. One newspaper headline screamed in all capital letters, "CLASE Y PODER," or, "Class and Power." An overflow crowd of 27,000-plus crammed into Estadio Monterrey, and adoring fans were everywhere, cheering his every move.

"My first impression in trying to describe it," Gebhard said at the time, "is that Vinny is somewhere between Abraham Lincoln, John F. Kennedy, and Babe Ruth."

A tough act to live up to, as Castilla discovered.

"I was coming off the best year of my career," Castilla said. "But I put pressure on myself that day because everybody wanted me to hit a home run. I tried so bad to hit one, but I didn't—but we won the game. That stadium was packed. They even added extra lights. It was a great experience."

HAPPY RETURN I

You can call Castilla a product of Coors Field if you like—you wouldn't be the first. That was an often-heard criticism back in the pre-humidor days, and during Castilla's run of success from 1995-1999. After that he went to three other teams in a three-year span, and couldn't come close to matching his production with the Rockies.

So why did the Rockies trade him, anyway—especially when all they got in return were Rolando Arrojo and Aaron Ledesma?

"His contract was getting to the point where it was up in the $7-, $8-, $9-million a year area, and we just couldn't afford that," O'Dowd said. "So we were motivated to move him because of the financial situation. He's probably the one that in hindsight I should have waited on for a year. He just performed so well in this ballpark. And he's such a good guy, as I've gotten to know him. I never really grasped the affinity for those (Blake Street Bombers)."

The day he was traded, December 13, 1999, was one Castilla would rather forget.

"When I left here the first time, I thought I would never come back," he said. "I didn't want to leave. I had my house here. That was a sad day. I heard rumors near the end of that season that it might happen. I didn't go in there and say, 'Don't trade me.' If they didn't want me here anymore, I wasn't going to say anything.

"Tampa, I was miserable there. I got hurt and they wanted me to keep playing because they were paying me a lot of money. The second year, they benched me after 30 at-bats. They said I couldn't help them anymore. Finally, they released me and I went to Houston and had a great year there."

After two solid seasons back in Atlanta, Castilla returned to Colorado in 2004—four seasons after he left—and wouldn't you know it, he hit 35 homers and led the league with 131 RBIs at age 37. What is it about Coors Field that brought out the best in him?

"That year, I had more home runs on the road—21 road, 14 here," Castilla said. "But I love this ballpark. It's beautiful. I love coming here every day. It's a good place to play. Good place to hit."

HAPPY RETURN II

Castilla got one last chance in a Rockies uniform at the end of the 2006 season, when after being released by San Diego he was brought back for a farewell tour in the final six weeks of the season.

His last day in a Rockies uniform, at least as a player, is one he will never forget. Before the game, everywhere you looked in the home clubhouse at Coors Field, players were wearing T-shirts that looked like Rockies jerseys, complete with Castilla's No. 9 on the back. On a sun-splashed Sunday in late September, he couldn't duplicate the past in an 0-for-4 game, but that didn't matter to a crowd of 30,216 who cheered his every move.

"I was so nervous and excited that morning, I didn't even want to eat," Castilla said. "That was beautiful. What came to my mind playing that game were a lot of memories . . . when we clinched the playoffs in '95 . . . the first year I got 40 homers and 100 RBIs.

"I'll always remember when Todd (Helton) sent my son Marco over to me before the start of the fifth inning, to give me third base. That base is in our home now. I started crying that day. Everybody was grabbing me and hugging me and telling me what a great career I had. I just couldn't control it."

MR. NICE GUY

Burks spent almost five full seasons in a Rockies uniform—his membership as a Bomber fluctuating with his health.

He came fairly inexpensively as a free agent in the winter between the 1993 and 1994 seasons, in part because of previous injury issues. And sure enough, Burks stayed healthy enough to play in only 145 games during his first two seasons in Colorado, both years being interrupted by a lingering wrist injury that required surgery.

But for one glorious season, 1996, Burks was a Bomber with the best of them. Burks led the league in runs (142), slugging percentage (.639), total bases (392), and extra base hits (93). He also was second in the league in batting average (.344), hits (211), and doubles (45). Oh, and on the side he hit 40 homers, stole 32 bases, made the All-Star team, won a Silver Slugger Award, and finished third in the Most Valuable Player Award vote.

"Ellis could hit a fastball, and don't hang a slider to him either," Baylor said. "The thing about him was the quickness of his bat. He needed some special handling when it came to his health. We tried to keep him on the field, but sometimes he needed a day (off). Especially during his big year, the guys all pushed Ellis, trying to keep him on the field. They knew how valuable he was to our team."

Added Hurdle: "Ellis Burks, at times, hit the ball as hard to right-center as left-handed pull hitters. And he was one of the best high-ball hitters I ever worked with or saw."

Burks offered two other rare advantages: he put up those kinds of numbers while playing center field and hitting in the No. 2 spot in the lineup, behind Young and in front of the rest of the Bombers.

"In the National League, where you usually have situational guys moving runners, hitting behind guys, bunting, we had Ellis—this beast—hitting second," Weiss said.

Burks put together another formidable season in 1997—.292, 32 home runs, 82 RBIs in 119 games—and was well on his way to another in 1998, when he was traded before the July 31 deadline to the Giants for Darryl Hamilton and two minor-leaguers. What never changed throughout his stay was Burks being as popular a teammate as anyone in the clubhouse.

"He was a quiet leader, another guy who related well with everybody," Bailey said. "He was very well respected. We had a number of guys like that. There weren't any cliques on that team. We had guys who bridged the subgroups in the clubhouse, Ellis was one; Cat, too.

"When Ellis was healthy, he was almost the same kind of player as Walker. What a talent. People don't realize how fast he was. First to home, scoring from second on a base hit, he could run with anybody."

FROM THE BEGINNING

It sounds a bit funny now that more than a decade has passed and the name "Helton" is atop virtually every important statistical category in Rockies history. But every star player was once a nervous rookie walking into a big-league clubhouse for the first time. For Helton, that day was August 1, 1997, at Three Rivers Stadium in Pittsburgh.

"I remember being in the cab from the airport, coming over the hill and seeing the city," Helton recalled. "I was so nervous about being late. I remember walking in and Walt Weiss really making me feel at home—typical Walt Weiss.

"I was a little intimidated. You respect the guys who were there. That was when Larry was going through his MVP season. The second game I played in, he hit a couple of doubles and a home run. It was impressive to watch.

"They still had Galarraga, Bichette, Vinny, and Ellis Burks. I was just trying to fit in. I felt lucky to be in that lineup. I wasn't really a part of it yet. I just tried to stay under the radar, keep my mouth shut, and play hard when they put me in there."

That first time was the following day, August 2, and due to Galarraga's presence, Helton played left field. His debut was fitting for what was to follow, and needless to say, he never went back to the Minor Leagues.

"I was really nervous during my first at-bat, but in a good way," Helton said. "I've probably never been so focused. I got a hit, made an out, got another hit, walked, then hit a home run to put us ahead in the game to right-center. That was pretty neat. Then I hit a home run the next day. I don't care how confident or cocky you are, there's always that doubt until you actually go out and do it. It always helps to be successful early."

Things have turned out OK since then, too. It takes 15 pages of the team's media guide to chronicle all of Helton's accomplishments. He is the franchise's all-time leader in games, at-bats, runs, hits, home runs, RBIs, total bases, doubles, on-base percentage, extra-base hits, multi-hit games, sacrifice flies, walks, and intentional walks.

Five All-Star Game appearances, three Gold Gloves, a batting title, and career numbers that rival first basemen of any generation, they're all on Helton's resume now. He has passed the 300-homer mark, and no player in history ever put together 10 consecutive seasons with 35 or more doubles until he did it. The nervous rookie has turned into the franchise player.

"If he's not the best player we've ever had, he's 1A," Hurdle said. "Since Walker left, Todd has been the face of the organization. He's made a lot of noise since his rookie year. Individually, there's not a lot more for him to accomplish. Just about anything he has set his mind to, he has been able to accomplish. He truly has a great game face. There are players you see who laugh and smile during the game, but him, no. He has a great game face."

And to younger players such as Holliday, Helton is the example-setter, the one everybody looks to in the clubhouse.

"When it's time to play ball, Todd's ready; he's prepared. And he expects you to be prepared as well," Holliday said. "He sets the bar high as far as going out and playing when you're nicked up. Whether you feel great or you don't, the expectation is for you to get out there and give it everything you've got, because you know that's what he's doing.

We know he expects us to bring it every night, and we don't want to let him down."

HIGHWAY ROBBERY

With Galarraga gone, Helton's long run as the everyday first baseman began in 1998, when everything went right—at least until after the season. Helton hit .315 and led the majors with a .398 average in August, when he also drove in 29 runs, and only three National League rookies in the previous 25 years hit more homers than his total of 25.

But as part of a repeating pattern when it comes to Rockies hitters, award voting didn't go his way. In the closest Rookie of the Year vote in years, the Cubs' Kerry Wood, who struck out 20 in one game and 233 in 166 innings, and who won 13 games with a 3.40 ERA, won the award. Helton finished a close second. Should he have won?

"Yeah, probably, but I don't want to say that," Helton said. "(Wood) was good that year. He still is."

But Siegle certainly would say it: "You talk about robbery? That was robbery. Todd should have won, but they gave it to Kerry Wood, mostly because he struck out 20 guys in one game. But for overall excellence over the course of a year?

"Yeah, Todd was playing at Coors Field, but so what? You still have to hit the damn ball. A lot of guys play in Coors Field, but they can't even *say* Rookie of the Year, let alone qualify for it. He was robbed. That's all there is to it. I've always believed that."

A YEAR FOR THE AGES

Helton's 2000 season was so good, it almost defied logic. He won the batting title with a .372 average and flirted with the .400 mark as late as August. He led the league with 216 hits. He led the league with 147 RBIs. He led the league with 405 total bases. He led the league with a .698 slugging percentage. He led the league with a .463 on-base percentage. He led the league with 59 doubles. And he hit 42 homers and scored 138 runs, too.

"It's the greatest year any Rockies player will ever have," O'Dowd said. "I have no doubt that that year will never be duplicated."

In fact, why stop with just the Rockies: only Babe Ruth, Lou Gehrig, Jimmie Foxx, and Hank Greenberg ever had seasons of at least 200 hits, 40 homers, 100 RBIs, 100 extra-base hits, and 100 walks. Nobody had ever done it in National League history. Only Ruth, Gehrig, and Rogers Hornsby ever had such a high batting average with that many homers. And Helton's 59 doubles were the most in the majors in 64 years.

"The only other time I've seen anything close to that was Albert Belle in 1995, when he basically took that team to the World Series," Bell said.

Just don't expect Helton to get carried away talking about it.

"It was one of those things where everything went right," he said. "I never got into a slump. Mentally, I was as sharp as I've ever been. Basically, I didn't try to do too much, and it worked out. That was a good year. But it was stressful at the end. I started jumping rope in my own head there, as far as trying to hit .400. I put a little bit too much pressure on myself."

ROCKY TOP

Even after a player has been in the Major Leagues for 11 seasons, making a projection of his final career numbers is a dicey proposition.

Todd Helton displays the Silver Bat from his 2000 season, a year that isn't likely to be matched. *AP Images*

Injuries can strike, diminished production is inevitable, and trades can occur, putting players in entirely different home-ballpark settings.

And in fact, the first two factors have already come into play with Helton, doing some damage to his legacy. In 2005, he spent two weeks on the disabled list, and his numbers fell to .320, 20 homers, and 79 RBIs—all career lows up to that point.

In 2006, Helton was sidelined by a bout with acute terminal ileitis, an intestinal ailment that landed him in Rose Medical Center for three days. He missed 17 games and came back too soon, playing at less than 100 percent the rest of the way, and the numbers dipped further to .302, 15 homers, and 81 RBIs—something for which O'Dowd takes some blame.

"I should have stepped in with him, and said, 'You are not being activated. You are going to stay on the disabled list until you get all of your weight back, until you get all of your strength back,'" O'Dowd said. "I wanted him back, selfishly, because he's such a great player. Even when he's not 100 percent healthy, he's better than 90 percent of the players out there."

Back problems also have been a periodic issue, and the special circumstance in Helton's case is the documented drop in offense at Coors Field as a result of the humidor. But bottom line, there is no getting around the fact that the Helton who performed from 1997-2004 was on a direct path to Cooperstown, but the one whose career numbers include the last three seasons is a Hall of Fame longshot.

Putting the final numbers on Helton's ledger is merely a projection at this point. Nonetheless, from the 2007 Bill James Handbook comes these projected career totals for Helton: .321 batting average, 2,924 hits, 722 doubles, 443 home runs, 1,641 RBI, 1,708 runs, .424 on-base percentage, .555 slugging percentage, 1,612 walks, 1,289 strikeouts. James also estimates Helton's chances of reaching 3,000 hits—an automatic Hall of Fame accomplishment to date—at 19 percent.

How accurate will those be? There's no way of knowing at this point. But as Hurdle says, "Todd is to the point where you start looking at those kinds of things."

If you judge a player by the company he keeps, you must be impressed with a guy who for a little while was the best quarterback at the University of Tennessee, keeping Peyton Manning on the sideline.

Helton entered 2007 as one of five players with a .330 career batting average, .400 on-base percentage and .590 slugging percentage. The other four? Babe Ruth, Ted Williams, Lou Gehrig, and Albert Pujols.

He also entered 2007 with the highest batting average among active players at .333, with only Williams and Tony Gwynn posting higher marks since World War II. And Helton is the only player in history to hit at least .315 with 25 homers and 95 RBIs in each of his first seven seasons. And when you compare Helton's numbers with the 18 Hall of Fame first basemen, he is in the top five in several major categories. There's more, but you get the point.

"This guy is a superstar," O'Dowd said. "He's one of the best hitters I've ever seen."

6

1996–1999: UNFULFILLED EXPECTATIONS

200-200

The biggest misconception about the Blake Street Bombers' glory days is that they were nothing more than mashers who benefited from playing at altitude. All you have to do to dispel that notion is look at the numbers from 1996, when the balance of power and speed was overwhelmingly efficient.

The Rockies crossed the plate 961 times that season, and no team in history ever scored more runs at home than their total of 656, or 8.1 per game. They hit their home runs—221 in all. But this offense was in motion to the tune of a club-record 201 stolen bases, enough to lead the league for the only time in franchise history.

Two-hundred-plus homers, 200-plus steals, a dozen years after the fact, the man behind it all, Baylor, proudly says, "Nobody's done it since.

"After 1995, I came back with a different kind of philosophy for Coors Field," Baylor said. "At that time, guys were getting away from taking (pregame) infield and outfield.

"I said, 'OK guys, this is what we're going to do. We're going to tag up on every ball. The reason? Guys don't throw anymore. We can catch guys flat-footed. We can take the extra base, stay out of double plays. Guys who can't run, we'll work on leads. I'll pick a pitch, one I think is going to be a breaking ball.' Then they'll go."

Just over a quarter of those 201 steals came from Young, who swiped 53 in a career year in which he wrestled the Silver Slugger Award away from Houston's Craig Biggio, who—ironically enough—the Rockies heavily pursued as a free agent the previous winter.

As for the Bombers: Burks' career year included 32 stolen bases to go with a .344 average, 40 homers, and 128 RBIs. There was a 31-homer/31-steal season from Bichette, and both Walker and Galarraga stole 18 bases.

Walker's total would have been much higher, but he played in only 83 games after suffering a fractured clavicle running into the wall on June 9, bringing to an end his experiment with center field. But that just allowed McCracken to chip in 17 steals.

"That was fun, watching guys do some things they probably hadn't done before, or had the liberty to try," Baylor said.

SHOOTING BLANKS

For all the Rockies' slugging exploits in 1996—and the list goes on and on—they were victims of no-hitters not once but twice that season. Never before and never since, but twice in 1996.

This was the season three Bombers hit 40 or more homers. The Rockies also had the league leader in homers and RBIs (Galarraga), runs and slugging percentage (Burks), and stolen bases (Young). But none of those exploits came against the Marlins' Al Leiter on a sunny May 11 in Florida, or against the Dodgers' Hideo Nomo on a rainy September 17 in Coors Field.

CUTTING TO THE CHASE

It was a muggy Saturday afternoon and the Rockies were in the midst of another of their miserable trips through Atlanta and South Florida. They had already been swept by the Braves in a three-game series, and lost the series opener to the Marlins when they ran into Leiter and his dominating cut fastball.

The Marlins scored six runs in the first inning, three on Charles Johnson's long home run, to remove all the drama in an 11-0 whitewashing, and Leiter took care of the rest. He needed only 103 pitches to complete his masterpiece, walking two batters and hitting another while striking out six.

The Rockies' only scoring threat came in the second, when Galarraga walked and Burks was hit by a pitch. A strikeout and a double-play ground ball ended that inning, and after Jayhawk Owens walked to lead off the third, nobody else reached base. With the help of two double plays, Leiter faced only 28 hitters.

"I remember that I said, 'How could Al Leiter throw a no-hitter against us?'" Baylor said. "He was mad at me about that. He just kept throwing that cutter in on everybody's hands, and they couldn't lay off. Batter after batter, and nobody ever made an adjustment. Every team I've been on, they've had trouble in Florida. Guys think they're going to Hawaii or something, lounging out by the pool (at the hotel). Then there's nobody in that ballpark."

NOMO'S NO-NO

How unlikely and unexpected was Nomo's no-hitter—still the only one in Coors Field history? Let's count the ways:

The Dodgers' earlier trip to Coors Field that season was for the infamous Slugfest Series, when both teams combined to bat .378 with 25 home runs and 17 doubles. The Dodgers' starting pitcher in that 16-15 marathon was none other than Nomo, who allowed nine hits and nine runs in five innings. The Rockies stole 10 bases in that game, nine of which came when Nomo was on the mound.

But the night of September 17 was like few others at Coors Field. Heavy showers forced a rain delay of two hours. Did the added humidity help Nomo's dive-bomb of a split-finger fastball? Most likely it did. And to improve his footing on a wet mound, he pitched from the stretch most of the game.

The Rockies got two runners to second base, both on stolen bases following two of Nomo's four walks. Their last baserunner was Young, who drew a leadoff walk in the sixth, and was promptly caught stealing. Meanwhile, the Dodgers struck for nine runs and 14 hits against Swift and three relievers, and the game ended on a strikeout of Burks, Nomo's eighth.

"Nomo, that one still ticks me off," Baylor said. "It was raining, so there was no BP. Plus, you're sitting around in the clubhouse for two hours during the delay. Guys are playing cards. I didn't like guys playing cards in the clubhouse. I got that from Gene Mauch. He didn't like it either. Guys lose their edge.

"So now the game finally gets going, and before you know it, it's the seventh inning and he has a no-no on the board. There was nothing close or questionable. He was throwing that split in the dirt, and guys kept swinging at it. The (previous) time we faced him, we tried to run him out of the park."

ROAD KILL

The flip side to the Rockies' smashing success in Denver was always the 81 games away from home each season. The dichotomies in terms of won/loss records and offensive statistics were staggering in the pre-humidor days.

The best the Rockies did in any season on the road was in 1995, when they went 33-39 in a shortened season. They bottomed out at 28-53 the following year, and were consistently in the 32-36-win range for the rest of the Bombers era.

"Back then, pitching in Denver was about 50 percent of the game, and pitching in all the other parks was about 75 percent of the game," McMorris said. "We could win at home in those slugfests, but we couldn't win on the road to save our necks."

O'Dowd touched on a more subtle dynamic that he witnessed early in his regime.

"It's very difficult to create a fundamental team environment when you can do things outside of the fundamental team approach and they work," he said. "Meaning, you can take a 3-1 pitch that is a little up, a little off the plate, and still hit it out of the ballpark (at Coors Field). And then you go out on the road and take that same approach, and you fail."

Don Baylor's power-and-speed style of offense was a perfect fit in pre-humidor Coors Field. *AP Images*

In 1995, the Rockies hit .316 at home and .247 on the road, and the runs scored differential was 485 to 300. Compare that to 1996, their most schizophrenic season: .343 batting average and 656 runs scored at home, .228 batting average and 303 runs on the road.

The next three seasons were near-duplicates, with home batting averages in the .321-.325 range, away batting averages ranging from .248 to .257, and an average run differential of just more than 200 per season, or 2.5 runs per game.

There was no fighting the reality of how difficult it was for everybody, especially hitters, to transition between the radically different conditions at Coors Field and everywhere else around the game. And after a long homestand, the Rockies always embarked on a road trip with a burned-out bullpen.

"We struggled so dramatically on the road," Hurdle said. "We weren't performing at all on the road, with the same guys who had just crushed the ball at home. You get so frustrated, you try to think of anything. We had all kinds of different thoughts. But those were all Band-Aids, because it came down to the fact that the dynamics were just different and we weren't making adjustments."

Added Dipoto: "We had to learn to play one way at home and another way on the road. The adjustments for the other 29 teams were pitch-to-pitch, out-to-out—in-game adjustments.

"But at Coors Field both offensively and for the pitchers, you had to make muscle-memory adjustments, too. Every seven or 10 days, you'd have to re-teach your body where your arm angle should be. You take our team with Darryl Kile, and dump it in Cincinnati, and it probably would have won 90 games. But the element of playing at Coors Field caused so much trouble."

Making matters worse, the Rockies left home to face media and fan criticism. Writers said Rockies hitters were mostly a product of their environment. Opposing fans mocked them.

"A couple of times, I stopped the guys from taking BP on the road," Baylor said. "They would get into bad habits trying to hit home runs in BP, just to prove everybody wrong. They would hear it all the time: 'You guys can't hit on the road. You're just Coors Field hitters.'"

And at times, the Rockies believed it.

"We'd be on the road, and things would start to go bad. You know how things would snowball," Helton said. "Some guys would say, 'Oh, my swing is screwed up right now. I know I can get it fixed when we get back to Coors Field.'

"I know that went through guys' heads, and 90 percent of it was mental. I never thought like that. If I feel there is something wrong with my swing, I'm fixing it, even if it's between at-bats. I'm not waiting until we get back to Coors Field."

In his one-year stay, Leyland recognized the obvious and tried to change the roster's makeup to compensate.

"At our place, it was almost like a slow-pitch softball game," Leyland said. "That's not a criticism. That's just a fact. We had a bunch of sluggers, a bunch of flyball-hitting guys. Some of those balls the Bombers hit that were out at Coors Field, were caught on the road. We didn't have many other ways to manufacture runs. We couldn't take the extra bases.

"Larry Walker was the best base-runner I've ever seen, but other than him, we really didn't have any speed. Our defense wasn't any good. Geb and I talked about that. We needed speed somewhere to go with the power."

Kind of sounds like the formula for the record-setting offense in 1996, doesn't it?

BAYLOR'S LAST HURRAH

But by 1998, when the Rockies slipped back below .500 after three consecutive winning seasons, Baylor's ways were questioned more and more, especially by Gebhard.

To anyone who was around them, it was hardly a secret that these two proud, strong-willed (OK, stubborn) longtime baseball men butted heads on issues. Gebhard questioned Baylor's in-game moves; Baylor didn't appreciate Gebhard's looming clubhouse presence. And each had their factions of support within the organization.

"There was petty stuff going on between the Geb guys and the Baylor guys," McMorris said. "When things weren't going good, you felt that more. That was an ongoing thing. That was no secret."

McMorris put a stop to the idea of letting Baylor go during the 1998 season—not with the Rockies playing host to the All-Star Game that July. But near the end of the season, Baylor knew his time was almost up.

"I've been around when other managers were fired," he said. "(In Anaheim) Gene Autry's favorite was (Jim) Fregosi. But then Gene didn't come around, and Fregosi was gone. (Owners) stop coming around.

"We were in Pittsburgh for three days late that season, and the owners were there, too. Nobody came into the clubhouse. They stayed in their box all series. Neifi (Perez) hit a home run that last day of the season, and we won. But when Geb said, 'Meet me in the hotel downtown,' I knew that was my last hurrah."

Baylor's final log: 440 wins, 469 losses, and a .484 winning percentage—the latter still tops among the club's four managers. And he did it with an expansion roster built from scratch.

"I hated to lose Don," McMorris said. "We tried to keep him as a vice president in the organization, but he made the decision that he wanted to stay on the field. And I understand why he made that decision. For the longest time, he was the only one who got us to the playoffs, and isn't that what it's all about?"

LEYLAND'S LAMENT

The deal went down at Leyland's Pittsburgh-area home, and in his words, "There wasn't a lot of dickering. It was pretty simple."

The disappointing 1998 season had barely concluded when the Rockies brass—Gebhard, McMorris, Charlie and Dick Monfort—went east to get their man. Talks moved so quickly that Leyland felt compelled to call another suitor and tell them he was headed west. A three-year deal was struck, just in time to get everybody involved on the flagship station KOA back in Denver that same night, October 5.

"Everyone was in a very celebratory mood," said the show's host, Lou from Littleton.

And with good reason. This was a match both sides wanted. The longtime successful manager and World Series champion, his team sold out from under him in Florida, looking to relocate; and the franchise that was the envy of others in many ways, flush with cash, with a great ballpark in a baseball-crazy environment.

But almost as quickly as the deal was reached, things unraveled to the point where the 1999 season remains the low point in franchise history: the dismal disappointment of a 72-90, last-place finish, and Leyland, frustrated and unhappy, walking away from the remaining two years and more than $4 million on his contract.

There are many theories as to what went wrong, and why, each with varying degrees of merit:

•The Columbine tragedy occurred on April 20 and for months cast a pall over the entire region, let alone the fortunes of the local major-league baseball team. The tragedy also changed the minds of the Leyland family on moving to Colorado. They stayed in Pittsburgh, forcing Leyland to spend part of the season living in the Coors Field clubhouse, and to visit nearby establishments late into the night.

•Leyland thought the club was better than it actually was—especially the pitching—as young starters John Thomson and Jamey Wright proved that they weren't ready for a big-league rotation. Then there was the issue of Gebhard in effect being a lame duck, unable to improve the roster, as Leyland expected would occur.

•Leyland didn't get along with some of his players, and his style of play was the antithesis of what was necessary to be successful at Coors Field. The Rockies just pulled out the lumber and mashed; Leyland preferred little ball, and back in his Pirates days, had No. 2 hitter Jay Bell lay down 69 sacrifice bunts in a two-year span.

What there is no debating about is that the supposed right man for the job—the man who managed a world champion in Florida in 1997 and got Detroit to the 2006 World Series—was all wrong for Colorado. In his typically no-nonsense, brutally honest, and self-flagellating style, here is how Leyland looks back at it:

"I want to make this perfectly clear: everybody in that organization—Jerry McMorris, the Monforts, Keli McGregor, Geb—made it as nice as humanly possible for me there. And I just didn't do the job. To this day, I'm embarrassed about it. It is the most embarrassing moment of my career. And that was really one of the reasons why I came back (to manage the Tigers).

"The fans were coming out. The team was getting an identity. Don Baylor had done a good job. They tried to do everything they could to treat me right. But my style wasn't working. I was frustrated. I tried. It wasn't like I gave up or anything. I wasn't getting through to the

players. I didn't attack things the way you need to attack them. It just wasn't working.

"I'm still embarrassed about it, because I know how much confidence Jerry and Geb had in me. I know I disappointed them. They thought they were getting a good, veteran manager. I just didn't do a good job. That's the way it was. It is a wonderful place, a beautiful city. The ballpark is gorgeous. But it just didn't work.

"A lot of people got on me for it. I paid for it for a long time. But it wasn't like I was taking money. I gave two years back. I wasn't going to go back there, feeling the way I was, for two more years, taking the money. To be honest with you, at the time, I didn't think I'd ever manage again. I was burned out.

"We did look at homes out there, and then we decided that we didn't want to move. I don't think (the Columbine tragedy) had much to do with it at all. I don't. That would be a cop out on my part. It was just different there than what I was used to. It was just a mistake; one that I'll always regret.

"I've always felt that if I could have done a bang-up job out there, maybe Geb would still be there. Maybe Jerry would still be involved. I think Geb was in trouble before I got there. I'm not going to say that him getting fired was totally my fault. But if I had done a bang-up job, maybe they'd still be there. That's the reality of it.

"I've always prided myself on handling pitching. But when I was there, I didn't think the pitcher had a chance. I guess it's different now (because of the humidor), and that's good. So it probably was unfair to (expect much from) Wright and Thomson. A lot of pitchers weren't ready for Colorado. It was a rough place for any pitcher.

"As a manager, you sense if you're getting through to players or not, and what the atmosphere is you're creating. You can sense if it's not working. And when you feel that, you feel like a failure. I won't say ego, because I don't think I've ever had an ego. But I always had a certain

---

Jim Leyland calls his failed one-year stay in Colorado the most embarrassing time of his career. *AP Images*

amount of pride in the fact that I could handle a big-league club. But I just couldn't get through to them. I couldn't create the kind of atmosphere I was trying to create.

"The players were good guys, but there was some stuff going on. There were some jealousies. But that goes on with every club. That's what the manager is supposed to do; somehow get through all of that. And I didn't do it.

"When I didn't do a good job, that made them uneasy, and it made me uneasy. So people might get the impression we didn't get along, but that wasn't the case. I also think some of those guys thought I would come in and wave a magic wand, and we'd win. But it doesn't work that way. Of all people, I know that. This is a players' game.

"I've quit beating myself up over it, but in reality, there are two reasons why I came back—one is that I was with the Cardinals for those six years (after leaving Colorado), and I saw that it could be done. I saw what Tony (La Russa) was doing, players were buying into the program, and it was such a great place to be around that I got the itch again.

"The other reason is that in my heart, I didn't want my career as a manager to end that way. When you go out after 12-15 years managing in the big leagues, it should be a nice moment. But that was a sad moment. I don't feel like I was part of that organization, and it's nobody's fault but mine. I still feel part of the Pirates. I feel part of the Marlins. And now I feel part of the Tigers. But I don't feel a part of the Rockies. I guess I just didn't give it the chance.

"The last day (of the 1999 season) was very cold, and I don't mean the weather. Everybody knew I wasn't coming back. There was a cold feeling. There was no real warmth, from my side or theirs. Dan (O'Dowd) was new. We didn't really know each other. But I know Jerry was disappointed, and I don't blame him.

"It was a messed up year, and I helped mess it up. I got caught up in the fact that I really liked Jerry, and I really liked Geb. If I had really thought about working for friends like them, I probably would have turned down the job. And I wish I had.

"I've had a couple of other opportunities to manage clubs for some very close friends, and I turned them down. That will never happen, because I know how much it hurts me to have let Jerry and Geb down. That's not a good feeling to have to live with, but you have to just say: I did the right thing by not going back. If I could do it differently, I never would have taken the job because of those friendships."

ANOTHER SAD ENDING

As the 1999 season was unfolding in all its wrenching disappointment, more change was in the air. McMorris' confidence in Gebhard had waned, and in fact, Gebhard didn't make it through that year—gone before Leyland departed.

Gebhard had built a winner from scratch, but couldn't sustain it. The signing of Darryl Kile didn't work as expected, the deal for Mike Lansing blew up in Gebhard's face, and there was no second trip to the post-season in sight.

"The general rule is that a general manager gets two field managers, and Geb had had his two," McMorris said. "Things were going in the wrong direction. We still had exceptional fan support, and it was time to let somebody else see if they could take it and go."

But that didn't make it any easier on everyone involved.

"You could tell the signs," Siegle said. "We closed out a homestand in August with another loss. And we all sat up in the general manager's box. It was always Geb at the far left, then me next to him, and then Pat (Daugherty), Dick (Balderson), and the others.

"So all the other guys cleared out, and the two of us are just sitting there, and I look over at Geb, and there's tears coming down his face. I saw that, and I thought: here's a man whose whole life is the Rockies. He put that club together before McMorris was even a factor. The successes on the field, the aesthetics of the ballpark . . . everything was Geb.

"I saw the tears coming down, and I just quietly patted him on the back and walked out. He probably knew that was going to be his last game, and as it turned out, it was. It was a sad moment. It was the end of an era. The Geb era. He was a mighty, mighty important factor in that whole franchise."

GEBHARD RETROSPECTIVE

Almost a decade after the fact, Gebhard sees his dismissal in a more understanding light, but it's still not an easy subject for him to address. "At the time, I was bitter," he said. "I wanted a chance, first of all, to finish out the season, which didn't happen. I got fired August 20—my wife's birthday. On a Monday, I got a call about 10 o'clock at night from Mike Klis. He broke the story—front page—that I was going to be fired.

"I went to the ballpark the next day and Jerry denied it, and said that I was going to finish out the year. On Friday, the team went to Chicago, and Jerry said to me, 'Why don't you stick around, not make the trip?' Then he called me in and said he wanted to make a change.

"I'd never been fired from anything in my life. I was disappointed by when it happened and how it happened. I would have liked to have had another year to work with Jim Leyland. That's one of the reasons he left, too. He was disappointed in what happened.

"They did what they felt they had to do. They did their homework and they hired Dan, who was very qualified for the job. I certainly had no ill feelings toward Dan. But if everybody thought that winning was just a matter of changing the guy at the top, well, they found out it's not that easy."

Gebhard's current duties with the Arizona Diamondbacks often bring him to Coors Field, where he still feels a connection to the franchise he helped raise from infancy.

"I do still look at it as my baby," he said. "I put so much into it. And the fact that Clint is still there. We had brought him in at the minor-league level, then to the Major Leagues as a coach. And Helton is still there. Some of the guys we signed when I was the general manager—Holliday, for one. You walk around Coors Field and still see some of the same employees who were there from the beginning, so there still are those ties."

THE "ONE-MORE-PLAYER" SYNDROME

In the four seasons that followed the Rockies' unexpected 1995 playoff appearance, they never finished higher than third place, and never got closer than seven games from first place at the end of a season. Their records: 83-79, 83-79, 77-85, and 72-90.

All despite the fact that few clubs were in a better position to win. The Rockies had a great ballpark that was filled to capacity every night, producing big-market revenues. They spent money and added key newcomers. When they signed Walker, George Steinbrenner was impressed enough to call McMorris and congratulate him.

Free-agent hitters around the game wanted to play for the Rockies. In the wake of two very similar contract offers, Craig Biggio chose to stay in Houston rather than sign with Colorado before the 1996 season. How close was Biggio to wearing a Rockies uniform?

"It was as close as you can get," he said. "That team was missing one thing—a leadoff hitter. And I love Colorado—the mountains, the views, everything about it. The organization was great. The stadium was new. The atmosphere there was great."

Added McMorris: "Biggio was one I thought we had. I wish we would have gotten him, because that would have saved us from the (Mike) Lansing era."

Eventually, the Rockies even attracted prime free-agent pitchers. Yet there was the unchanging pattern: great at home, bad on the road. And they never got over the hump to get back in the playoffs.

The home-road dichotomies were a major factor. Also, by 1999, Leyland said a bit of complacency may have taken root. Things were almost *too* comfortable for everybody, especially the much-revered Bombers.

"The fans got associated with some of those guys," Leyland said. "They were never going to let it go. That was their team. Sometimes, and I'm not saying this about that team in particular, the names still sound good but the drive is not there. It was a great place to play. The attendance was great. There was probably some hunger that wasn't there."

And as the Rockies found out, there is a risk in spending with no guarantee of success, in trying to add that "one more player" to get back to the playoffs.

"A lot of those guys got old together," Siegle said. "To pay star money to guys whose production was dwindling was a bad combination. We had some of our own young pitchers coming; some panned out and some didn't. We had (Todd) Helton break in as a young player through our system. But by and large, we lost draft choices by signing free agents, and didn't catch up. The young talent wasn't ready when those guys faded.

"By way of expectation, we had that one-more-player syndrome. One year it was (Darryl) Kile. We went after Biggio. We went after Kevin Brown. And after I left, they signed Hampton and Neagle. You get into traps when that happens. You spend too much money. You give out too long of a contract. You lose draft choices. It's a domino effect. And ultimately, it affected the club.

"But 1995 raised the bar of expectations. When we won that year, they expected us to win every year, and that really put a lot of pressure on us. It wasn't unfair. We all wanted to win. So we went out and signed players, spent a lot of money, traded a lot of talent, but still didn't win again. All of a sudden, you say, 'Wow, was that worth it? Should we have done it?'"

7

BLAKE STREET BUSTS

OUT OF CONTROL

When then-Chicago Cubs first baseman Mark Grace heard that right-hander Mike Harkey chose to sign as a free agent with the Rockies in 1994, he posed the question: "Why would you want to go some place where they don't have any gravity?"

Harkey went anyway, and his career circled down the drain shortly thereafter. Maybe he and others who followed should have listened to Gracie, because for an organization that stressed, ad nauseam, the need to draft, sign, and develop pitching, the Rockies, for all the wrong reasons, turned out to be a perfect example of why that theory was correct.

Injuries, off-the-field accidents, bouts of complete loss of control, acquisitions ending in expensive failures, even a tragic death—you name it, Rockies pitchers fell victim. It added up to an inordinate share of misfortune, especially for a team that plays its home games a mile above sea level.

"It all seemed to happen to pitchers," McMorris recalled.

It started right from the beginning. John Burke was the club's first choice in the 1992 amateur draft, and the script couldn't have been written any better: local product from Cherry Creek High School who went on to star at the University of Florida, with all the tools scouts desire.

For his first two minor-league seasons, Burke was on the fast track to the Rockies' rotation. But control issues and injury problems cost him most of the 1994 season, shoulder tendonitis interrupted his 1995 season, and during one painful big-league spring training he temporarily lost grasp of the strike zone.

Burke did eventually surface in the big leagues, but in parts of the 1996-97 seasons, the Rockies' first first-round draft choice bounced between the rotation, the bullpen, and the disabled list, finishing with a 4-6 record and 6.75 ERA in only 74⅔ innings. Injuries ended his career six years after he was drafted.

"Burke might have had better stuff than Nied, but that one spring he had the yips and couldn't throw strikes," Gebhard said. "He battled through all of that, and stayed up (in the Majors) for a couple of years. I give him credit for that, but then he came up with arm problems."

Ruffin also endured a baffling temporary loss of control that almost cost him his career. He eventually overcame it to become a bullpen force in the 1994-96 seasons, when he saved a total of 58 games, but after accumulating seven saves by mid-May in 1997, elbow problems put Ruffin on the disabled list for a month. He returned to make five more appearances, was shut down again, and never threw another major-league pitch. He was done before he turned 34.

"Ruffin was fabulous in 1995," McMorris said. "Tommy Lasorda told me later, 'Ruffin would come in, and we couldn't touch him.' I never dreamed that when he got hurt, that would be the end of it. You can look back and say: if Ruffin had stayed healthy, and if Nied had stayed healthy, would the franchise look different? But every franchise has to go through that."

Gebhard knew the club was throwing Nied in over his head in the 1993 season, but that was part of the plan.

"Our long-range plan was for David Nied to be our No. 1 pitcher the first year," Gebhard said. "Then each year after, we would sign a top free agent, and Nied would slide down to the No. 2 spot, the No. 3 spot. He was supposed to be a staple in the rotation."

But what nobody counted on were the injuries that kept

interrupting Nied's development. Ultimately, he suffered a torn ulnar collateral ligament, and was done at age 27. The final numbers: 46 games, 218⅔ innings, a 14-18 record, and a 5.47 ERA.

"I really felt in my heart that David was going to be 10-12-game winner," Gebhard said, "but he came up with a bad arm. Kevin Ritz came up with a bad arm after we signed him to a three-year deal and he had been such a horse. Ruffin, at the end, had an elbow that was bothering him, and then he shut it down. It wasn't abuse. It just happened. We just had some bad luck."

A FORGETTABLE DEAL FOR THE FANS

With the Rockies in the midst of setting an all-time single-season attendance record in 1993, McMorris felt the need for a gesture of gratitude to the fans. So he encouraged Gebhard to look for some pitching to help an expansion team that was a miserable 36-62 at the time.

And so, the worst trade in Rockies history was made: Andy Ashby and then-prospect Brad Ausmus for right-hander Greg Harris and left-hander Bruce Hurst.

Blame it mostly on the effects of playing at altitude. Ashby had his shining moments elsewhere during a career in which he won 98 games, but at altitude he "looked like a deer in the headlights," as McMorris succinctly put it. So he had to go.

Harris was a valued commodity after four-plus solid seasons in San Diego. But at altitude, nothing much ever went right for him, and when he was dealt away one-and-a-half years later, he left with a 4-20 record and a 6.60 ERA. Due to injuries, Hurst threw all of 8⅔ innings with the Rockies.

"At that time, Greg Harris was a hot name," Gebhard said. "Everybody wanted him. I talked back and forth with (then-Padres general manager) Randy Smith, but we just couldn't match up. One day, (assistant general manager) Walt Jocketty said, 'Would Randy have more interest if we were willing to take on Bruce Hurst's salary?' So I threw that at Randy, and we were able to make that trade. Without a doubt, that was one of my worst trades.

"Ashby had probably the best arm on our staff, but he really was bothered by pitching in the altitude. And with Ausmus, if you remember, we had Girardi, and at Triple-A we had Ausmus and Jayhawk Owens. Our staff was split as to who was going to be best between those two as the No. 2 catcher.

"As it turned out, Ausmus turned out to be an excellent defensive catcher, and Jayhawk should have been a good hitter if he hadn't gotten hurt. But the point was that we could afford to give up one of those two."

EXHIBIT A

In the first five years of their existence, the only time the Rockies saw a pitcher as good as Darryl Kile was when he was wearing an opposing jersey.

Reynoso was serviceable enough to win 12 games in 1993. Saberhagen and Swift had track records of success but were in their 30s when they were acquired—already riddled with arm troubles, and only finding more with the Rockies. Ritz won a franchise-record 17 games in 1996 despite a 5.28 ERA, but did it by subscribing to the oft-heard mantra at pre-humidor Coors Field: just allow one less run than the opposing starter.

When the Rockies signed Kile to a three-year, $21-million deal in November of 1997, he was in his prime at 29, coming off a 19-7 record and a 2.57 ERA with Houston. This was the bona fide ace to lead the staff—or so everybody thought.

Yes, there were concerns about Kile's devastating curveball losing some of its effectiveness at altitude. But everybody involved simply wasn't worried enough to squelch the deal.

"I thought he could pitch here," Gebhard said. "I brought that up with him before we signed him. I said, 'You've pitched here, you know how difficult it can be. Do you think you can overcome it?' And he said, 'Absolutely.' He saw it as a challenge. You saw it on the road sometimes. He would go out there and be lights-out. We signed the right guy, but

The Rockies thought they had signed an ace in Darryl Kile, but he couldn't adjust to pitching at that altitude. *AP Images*

he just struggled with the altitude."

Kile made his starts—67 of them in a Rockies uniform. And he pitched his innings—421 over two seasons. He was the workhorse the club envisioned, but not the ace in terms of results. Kile went 13-17 with a 5.20 ERA in 1998, when he set team records with 230.1 innings pitched and 14 strikeouts in one game. His record easily could have been reversed, as the Rockies scored one run or less in five of his losses.

But things regressed in 1999, when he went 8-13 with an unsightly 6.61 ERA and almost as many walks as strikeouts. That left Kile at 21-30 with a 5.92 ERA with the Rockies, and in the end, the man known as D. K. was the perfect Exhibit A—if he couldn't succeed at Coors, who could?

The final numbers before Kile's tragic death: at Coors Field: 11-15, 6.76 ERA, 95 walks, and 137 strikeouts; everywhere else: 122-104, 3.83

ERA, 823 walks, and 1,531 strikeouts.

"I wasn't in this job a week when Barry Axelrod—Darryl's agent—called me," O'Dowd said. "This is an agent who I respect, and he told me, 'You need to get him out of there. I'll work with you, but he doesn't want to pitch there anymore. He cannot handle it there anymore. He's done.' So I traded him to St. Louis."

And Kile won 20 games the very next season.

A PAIN IN THE BACK

Bailey threw back-to-back shutouts—still a club record—and was 5-1 in early May of 1997. Things were going so well that there was talk of a possible All-Star spot. His season leveled off after that, and he finished 9-10 with a 4.29 ERA in 191 innings, but at 26, his future looked promising.

"You put up those numbers now, and you would make a lot of money," Bailey said.

But as it turned out, he never pitched in another major-league game. The following spring, he was a passenger in a car driven by Munoz, and as they were returning to their condos after a workout they were rear-ended at a stoplight.

"It wasn't a big accident by any means," Bailey said. "In fact, I remember Ruffin drove by just after it happened and waved at us. But I remember sitting in the car, saying, 'Something's not right.' Then as I tried to get out of the car, I felt all kinds of pain. I fractured my vertebrae in two places.

"The doctor in Tucson said to shut it down for the year, but I said, 'That's not going to happen.' I tried rehabbing it, but it didn't get any better. I finally shut it down in extended spring training. I couldn't feel anything in my fingers. I couldn't find my control again. It stemmed from my vertebrae. When you're at this level, there is a fine line. It doesn't take much to bring your skill level down.

"And I think my state of mind at the time was to try to protect myself, try to protect my back. That opened up injuries to other parts of my body. My elbow started hurting. I tried to finesse my way through, and

I started losing command, and then everything spiraled."

ONE IN A MILLION

Doug Million was everything you could ask for in a No. 1 draft choice. A lanky left-hander with an even disposition, he was *USA Today*'s high school player of the year when the Rockies picked him seventh overall in the 1994 draft.

It was one spot higher than where they picked Helton the following year, two spots ahead of where Jeff Francis was selected in 2002, and the same spot as where Troy Tulowitzki was chosen in 2005. In fact, until Greg Reynolds was picked second overall in 2006, no Rockies player was ever picked earlier than Million.

The kid's numbers were staggering: pitching for Sarasota (Fla.) High, Million was 33-4 with 353 strikeouts in three years. He was 12-2 with a 1.49 ERA in his senior year, including a 16-strikeout performance in the state title game. True to his name, he signed for just under $1 million.

But just over three years later, Million was dead. Three weeks short of his 22nd birthday, he collapsed while running and died of complications from asthma. Instead of a golden arm for their future, the Rockies were left with honoring his memory by naming an award after him that annually goes to the organization's top minor-leaguer.

"Doug would have been a big-league pitcher," Gebhard said.

A PAIN IN THE NECK

Dipoto took over the closer role from Ruffin in 1997, and over the next year-plus, racked up 33 saves. But late in 1998, he developed a blood clot that traveled from his right shoulder to his right wrist, leaving his hand white as a napkin and cold to the touch. That started a spiral that culminated with his forced retirement three years later at age 32.

During the 1999 season, Dipoto started having back and spinal problems, and on the first day of spring training in 2000, he felt a stabbing pain in his left shoulder during a long-toss session. Despite that, he threw two scoreless innings in his first outing, good enough to draw compliments from pitching coach Mark Wiley.

"But I said, no, something isn't right," Dipoto said. "They sent me for an MRI, and I had herniated disks in my neck. I said, 'Give me the cortisone shots, whatever you have to do, to try to get through this.' But when the cortisone wore off, it was just getting worse, and my fastball had gone from pretty good to not-so-good.

"In Montreal one night, I lost the sense of where my arm was. I'm trying to hit the strike zone, and I'm bouncing balls on the carpet up there. Brent Mayne came out to the mound and said, 'Dude, throw a strike.'

"And I said, 'Believe me, that's the plan, but I don't know what's going on.'

Two hitters later, I threw a pitch and my head felt like it had popped off. I fell down on the ground, holding my neck. Doctors told me I had to have spinal surgery. I came back and pitched in September, ahead of what the doctors wanted, and I threw fine.

"But I went back to spring training in 2001, and on the first day of live batting practice I threw a pitch and fell down in pain. They had already put a plate in the back of my neck, and the doctor said he could extend it, but he also said, 'I can't imagine you having a comfortable rest of your life that way.' So that made it pretty easy for me (to retire)."

8

2000-2002:
CH-CH-CH-CHANGES

DEALIN' DAN

While the miserable, 92-loss 1999 season wound its way down, the interview process for Gebhard's successor was ongoing. The winner turned out to be somebody Gebhard had interviewed a year earlier for the role of player personnel director—and didn't hire. Ownership preferred longtime baseball man Gary Hughes at the time, but on September 20, 1999, Daniel J. O'Dowd took over the entire baseball operation, picking the job over a similar offer in Milwaukee. And one of the first opinions he sought was that of Leyland, the manager who was on his way out.

"I have a tremendous respect for Jim," O'Dowd said. "I tried to get an evaluation of where the club was at, where we were at as an organization, what changes he felt had to be made. He really thought there were a lot of things that should have been done, and in his mind we were pretty far away from being a championship-caliber organization."

O'Dowd sure took the idea of change to heart: in 44 days after the 1999 World Series, he made five trades involving 23 players—including the first four-team deal in 14 years—and "Dealin'" soon became part of O'Dowd's name.

Two Bombers were sent packing—Bichette to Cincinnati for Hammonds and Stan Belinda, and Castilla as part of the four-team, nine-player mega-deal, going to Tampa Bay for Rolando Arrojo and Aaron Ledesma. Jeff Cirillo and Scott Karl were also acquired from Milwaukee, who received Wright and Henry Blanco from the Rockies. Kile got a ticket out of town and a career reprieve, going to St. Louis along with Dave Veres and Luther Hackman for closer Jose Jimenez, relievers Manny Aybar and Rick Croushore, and infielder Brent Butler.

The need to clear some money from the payroll was a factor in that winter of transition. But it got to the point where it was hard to keep track of who was still on the team and who wasn't. The 2000 Opening Day roster listed only a handful of players from the one that opened the 1999 season, and O'Dowd wasn't anywhere near finished. During the 2000 season, he made seven more deals involving 22 players.

The revolving door confused and frustrated longtime Rockies fans, especially when nobody captured their hearts as the departed Bombers once had. It was now Walker and Helton and a bunch of constantly changing faces.

At least the results on the field were slightly better, as Bell—O'Dowd's hand-picked successor to Leyland—guided the Rockies to an 82-80 finish in 2000. Still, O'Dowd has second thoughts about his first year-plus on the job.

"If I could start the job all over, I would have taken 2000 to make my own evaluations," O'Dowd said. "Taken the 2000 season, which actually turned out to be a pretty good year for us, to not have made any moves, just given Buddy the club and let him make some evaluations.

"In hindsight, it was such a bad year in 1999. It was a very negative situation. Perhaps we should have taken another year to let things play out, and see if some (clubhouse) issues could have resolved themselves. The environment had gotten so bad that maybe the players got caught up in it a little bit, too."

PLAN A

Surprisingly, the highest-scoring season in Rockies history wasn't Bomber-dominated. Instead, it came in 2000, when Helton led an attack that racked up 968 runs, 1,664 hits, and a .294 batting average—

all marks that were the best in the Majors since 1930.

Helton's year was Ruthian, one of the best in any era, but Walker only played in 87 games due to an elbow injury that required surgery, and nobody else hit more than 20 home runs. In fact, the Rockies scored 62 more runs than their opponents, despite hitting 62 fewer homers.

This was a different kind of attack, one fueled by doubles, 59 by Helton and 53 by Cirillo, the first pair of National League teammates to top 50 in the same season. And led by Tom Goodwin's 55, the Rockies stole 131 bases. It all came about more by circumstance than by design.

"We felt we really needed to try to move Dante, that the mix of oil and water had gotten to the point where it wasn't working," O'Dowd said. "But there was absolutely no interest other than Jeffrey Hammonds. He was a speed guy. Then we had a huge hole to fill in center field, because we were dealing with a (minor-league) infrastructure that wasn't ready to supply anything at that time.

"The evaluation of Juan Pierre that I was given at the time was that he was far away from impacting the major-league club. So the only available center fielder for us to sign as a free agent was Tommy Goodwin. We needed players to play positions. We didn't have (young) players who were ready to play at that point."

Despite the winning season, Bell managed no fewer than 49 players on the merry-go-round of a roster. Whether you remember them or not—and odds are, you don't—Darren Bragg, Bubba Carpenter, Jeff Frye, Jeff Manto, Elvis Pena, and Carlos Mendoza all appeared that season. Among the 24 pitchers used, there were cups of coffee for Rigo Beltran, Giovanni Carrera, Craig House, David Lee, David Moraga, and Pete Walker.

"We had such a huge turnover of players," Bell said. "I knew that the 1999 team didn't play real hard—there were some chemistry issues going on—so I knew changes needed to be made. But the honeymoon period (with the fans) was over at that point, so the money wasn't coming in like it had been before. That's why there was less patience.

"2000 was a good year, but it wasn't good enough to where they were making the kind of money they thought they should be making—the kind of money they were used to making. So it became a real issue behind the scenes."

HAMPTON AND NEAGLE

The impatience of which Bell spoke reached its critical point in the winter between the 2000 and 2001 seasons, and it would have catastrophic effects on the Rockies for years to come—only nobody in the organization knew it at the time. They were too caught up in rampant optimism.

The Rockies were thinking big that winter, Alex Rodriguez big. The mega-star shortstop was a free agent, and was wined and dined by the Rockies before settling on a mind-boggling 10-year, $252-million deal with the Texas Rangers.

And that's when the Rockies decided to spend their money—$175 million of it—on Mike Hampton and Denny Neagle. If they thought they were one player short—a pervasive feeling for a handful of years following the 1995 playoff appearance—this time they came up with two.

Specifically: two accomplished left-handers who, on paper, gave the rotation exactly what it needed: an ace at the top and a solid innings-eater in the middle. In the meantime they were buying time for younger pitchers to develop. They didn't come cheaply, especially Hampton, who signed an eight-year, $120-million deal, the highest given to a pitcher at the time and more than double the four years and $55 million Neagle received.

Think about it this way: only eight years ago, the Rockies, who now characterize themselves as a small-to-mid-market franchise, were able to spend more money than anybody else in history on a free-agent pitcher and sign him away from the New York Mets. It's very difficult to imagine that scenario unfolding today.

"(Mets owner) Fred Wilpon was sick that they couldn't keep Mike," McMorris said. "He told me, 'Mike can't be more than a tick behind

Mike Hampton, left, jokes with Larry Walker. But his stay in Colorado was anything but pleasant. *AP Images*

Randy Johnson. And he's far younger. I think you got the top left-hander.'"

But this was a disaster waiting to happen, especially for the long-term financial health of the franchise. When the signings didn't translate into wins and fans in the seats, there was a huge price to pay. The question that must be asked is did ownership know it was putting the franchise's financial well-being at risk?

"There was no question that there was risk," McMorris acknowledged. "But there was also risk if we didn't do anything. The 2000 team still had a lot of electricity. We played exciting baseball, and we were much more athletic, and we were winning. But attendance was coming down already. And Arizona put the two big guys (Johnson and

Schilling) together, and that put a lot of pressure on us.

"We were very surprised Hampton even wanted to consider coming here. We had already struck out on Kevin Brown. We had been used by other big pitchers to negotiate their (new) contracts. (Roger) Clemens, he wasn't going to come here. We put feelers out on him, but his agent said he wasn't going to come. We weren't backing off what we needed to do to get pitching in here."

With that said, O'Dowd still regrets the Hampton and Neagle signings.

"We really thought Hampton could work out," he said. "We had concerns about the years (on the contract). But we thought we had a chance to get a guy who would pitch 220 innings, could win 15-18 games a year, and could give us a chance to develop our other pitching coming through the system.

"St. Louis and Chicago were right there with everything we were doing. We separated ourselves by offering the extra year. Jerry recognized how difficult it was going to be to get a pitcher of that caliber."

WHAT WENT WRONG

For the first half of the 2000 season, Hampton was everything the Rockies envisioned and more. He even went to the All-Star Game, the first Rockies pitcher to do so. And then all of a sudden, he lost his bread-and-butter sinking fastball, and the downward spiral began.

"One thing I never thought about coming into this job was how different the ball felt here (before the humidor)," O'Dowd said. "The ball was truly like a cue ball. And when Mike started experimenting with grips, he began to change his arm action to regain the sink that was a God-given gift that he completely lost.

"Look at it this way: you've done something your whole life naturally, and every time you threw it, it was there. You didn't have to create, you didn't have to think about it. It was pure muscle memory. And all of a sudden, you wake up and it's not there. You say to yourself, 'It's going to come back, it's going to come back.' And it doesn't come back, and you get your butt kicked, and you're a great competitor.

"Plus, the physical toll it took on him . . . he would say, 'Every time I pitch here I feel like I'm back in high school, and it's Saturday morning after Friday night football.' When you couple the physical part of this game with the mental part of where he was at, he just lost his confidence to pitch, and he became just another guy. There was no way he was going to survive here. I think now, with the humidor, he would have a much better chance."

Added Bell: "I just think it was Coors Field. There wasn't anybody as tough as Mike. But he got into a rut and couldn't get out of it. He never had to go through anything like that. He was trying to figure it out—the arm angle, throwing across his body. He got into a mechanical funk, where he was trying too many things instead of trusting his stuff.

"Mike is such a perfectionist, too, and that was part of the problem. All Mike wanted to do was win, and when he won, he didn't want to win 8-7 or 10-9. He wanted to win 6-0 or 6-1. He didn't understand giving up so many runs there. It just wore him out.

"You can't feel sorry for a guy making the kind of money he was making, but knowing him the way I do, I felt bad for him. He was the best competitive pitcher going at that time. Everybody wanted him."

Like Kile, Hampton's tenure lasted only two seasons. In 2001, he finished 14-13 with a 5.41 ERA after peaking at 9-2 on June 10. But also like Kile, the numbers deteriorated the following year—7-15 with a 6.15 ERA—as did his relationship with the media. The latter reached a low point when he physically threatened *Denver Post* columnist Mark Kiszla during a profanity-laced tirade after a Colorado Avalanche-Detroit Red Wings playoff game.

Somehow—and O'Dowd deserves credit for making it happen—the Rockies were able to unload Hampton (and at least part of the contract) after the 2002 season.

The Florida Marlins took him and Pierre, and dumped money of their own in the contracts of Charles Johnson and Preston Wilson. But it still took several seasons for the Rockies to be free of any financial obligations on Hampton.

Neagle didn't last much longer than Hampton, at least on the Rockies' active roster. His 2001-02 cumulative numbers were respectable for a flyball pitcher at altitude—17-19 with a 5.32 ERA. But seven starts into the 2003 season, Neagle developed serious arm troubles that led to ligament-replacement surgery.

He attempted comebacks but never pitched in another regular-season major-league game before an embarrassing off-the-field arrest led to the club trying to get out of what remained on his contract. An out-of-court settlement was reached, and Neagle's final totals with the Rockies were 19-23 with a 5.57 ERA in 72 games.

"Denny was a free spirit," Bell said. "He would have been fine, except he ran into injury problems."

Added O'Dowd: "In Neagle's case, won-loss-wise, he was one of the better starting pitchers on the market that winter. Health-wise, his history was not great but not awful, and we learned the year before that guys who threw strikes and had above-average change-ups had a chance to do well here.

"With Mike, Denny, and Pedro Astacio, we felt we were putting together a formidable starting rotation. The direction I was given was: we want to win, and we want to win now. My job was to try and make that happen."

PANIC IN DENVER

The unraveling of the relationship between Bell and O'Dowd reached a critical point during that 2001 season, when they butted heads on the course the team was taking. In essence, Bell thought ownership made the critical mistake of giving up too early after a slow start.

A six-game losing streak in late June was particularly costly. It dropped the Rockies below .500 at 36-38, 10 games behind first-place Arizona, and the next day they dealt away Brent Mayne for backup catcher Sal Fasano and right-hander Mac Suzuki, who flopped in a few big-league appearances.

Ben Petrick, long expected to be the franchise's next star position player after Helton, quickly proved he wasn't ready for everyday catching duties, and the Rockies' troubles worsened. A few years later, Petrick's battle with Parkinson's disease was revealed, another sad and inexplicably tough break for him and the franchise to endure.

Shortly after the All-Star break, Todd Walker was sent to Cincinnati for young outfielder Alex Ochoa, who never fulfilled his potential. And in the week leading up to the July 31 trade deadline, Bell was dealt the double whammy of losing the franchise's most successful pitcher up to that point—Astacio, who was sent to Houston for Scott Elarton—and Gold Glove-winning shortstop Perez for three minor-leaguers who surfaced only briefly.

It was a painful fall for a team that had sparked so much optimism only a few months earlier. Hampton's season began turning south after the All-Star break, and the Rockies followed his lead. They lost nine in a row, including six at home in late August, and by losing the last five games of the season, they finished 73-89, about the reverse of what was expected.

"We signed Mike and Denny, we were .500 in June, and talk about panic," Bell said. "A lot of the reason we signed Denny was to show Mike we were serious about contending. And we were. But what happened was, (the owners) became very impatient with being .500 in June. I mean, come on. I don't think there was any question that that team would have been pretty damn good before the year was out.

"But then we traded Mayne, we traded Astacio, Neifi, Todd Walker. Brent Mayne—that was not a good move. No doubt about it, they started trading off guys to save money. If you're going to sign a guy like Mike Hampton, then you better have a little bit more money to help him win.

"The problem was, they didn't have the resources. They had gone as far as they could (financially), and that's when it got real personal, and real serious. Everybody was talked about, as far as being traded—Walker, Helton, everybody. I don't know if that was a championship team, but it was too early to blow it up after three months. I loved our team. We had guys who played hard every night. They cared about each other.

"(The owners) knew my feeling on it, but their biggest concern was making money. That's their right, but did they really understand what their fans wanted? There's no doubt in my mind that if they had made smarter decisions, they would have made a lot more money in the long run.

"But there just wasn't the foresight that they weren't going to make $50 million every year, that every once in a while they were going to have to back up and understand how to build an organization, so that later on they could make the money back. The focus was on the right-now."

THE BELL TOLLS NO LONGER

The 2002 Rockies got out of the gate terribly, losing 15 of 19 after a 2-1 start, including two five-game losing streaks. In the midst of it all, Bell made up his mind that Denver wasn't the place for him to be.

"I got word that they were going to talk to me about an extension," Bell said. "And that's when I went to Keli and told him that I wasn't going to come back (after 2002). That was the second or third week of April. And a week later, I was fired. I don't know if that was written back then, but that's what happened.

"My relationship with Dan and ownership just wasn't a good situation for anybody, really. It got too personal. It just wasn't a good fit. We lost the last three games I was there, in Cincinnati. When we got back home, I got fired. Dan came down to my office and said, 'We're going to make a change.' It didn't surprise me.

"I wish it would have turned out differently, but there were things that were happening that I didn't like. They know why I didn't want to talk about an extension. And I did want to be extended at one point.

"A lot of it had to do with a young organization going through some tough times for the first time. There was no reason why they should have known how to handle it. I'm not blaming anybody, because you don't get better until you experience it. They learned from it, I'm sure.

"But you have to be patient to put a team together. And you have to

Buddy Bell thought management pulled the plug too early in 2001 by making mid-season trades. *AP Images*

hang on to the guys who are tough. You get these guys used to playing at Coors Field, and they understand the emotions of the game there, and then you bring somebody else in who doesn't understand it. You have to be a tough SOB to play there.

"I used to talk to Dan about it all the time. You just can't keep making change after change after change and be that impulsive. Then we got sideways and didn't see things eye to eye, and that's why people get fired."

Of O'Dowd's regrets about his first few years at the Rockies' helm, losing Bell ranks near the top.

"We got to a point where things didn't work out, and we had to do some things that were incredibly painful," he said. "Things weren't working, and as an organization we realized we had to shift gears.

"I always have felt bad about that. Buddy was a dear friend of mine. It didn't end the way a friendship should end. I wish I could have been a better friend to help him through the situation. It was a very emotional time. I'm sure I failed in my communication with him. You get in those situations where you don't know what to say, so you don't communicate."

9

THE HUMIDOR

IT HAD TO BE THE BOOTS

Tony Cowell had no idea he was about to make baseball history. He just hated how sore his feet were getting in his leather hunting boots.

With the 2001 season in the books, the electrician in the Coors Field engineering department dragged those boots out of the closet for a hunting trip to the mountains. Normally he would have treated them with a softening agent after a summer of non-use. But this time, he just grabbed them and headed to the Rocky Mountains, where he would hatch arguably the most important development in the history of the Rockies franchise.

"It was the first day out, there was nothing going on, I didn't see anything other than the beautiful mountain vistas," Cowell recalled, "and my boots were hurting my feet. They had shriveled up over the summer and got all dry. They were brittle and tight, and it was just one of those moments when something comes to you.

"I thought: a baseball is made out of leather, too. If my boots shrunk and dried out over the summer, was the same thing happening with baseballs? I didn't say a word to anybody I was with on the trip. But I couldn't wait to get off that mountain and tell somebody."

If baseballs were shrinking and getting as hard and slick as cueballs, as pitchers were constantly complaining, then why not store them in conditions where that could be prevented? McGregor was the first to hear of Cowell's theory, and gave the go-ahead for some testing.

"We took some new balls right out of the box, and compared them with balls that had been around here for a while—you know, old batting-practice balls," Cowell said. "You could feel a difference in weight, and I'm not even a pitcher. The old balls were smaller and harder.

"Then we dropped the two sets of balls from a high spot, about 30-40 feet above the ground, and there was a noticeable difference in how they bounced. The old balls bounced a couple of feet higher. It was enough for us to go ahead and start to put together the humidor."

Things never would be the same around Coors Field again.

"The humidor for me is the single greatest thing that's happened for this franchise since getting to the playoffs in 1995," O'Dowd said early in 2007. "It's as important as any player we've ever had because it's given us a chance to build a ball club where pitching matters. And I don't think you can win unless pitching matters.

"Before that, pitchers were an afterthought, and the focus was on the offensive ability of the club. For a scientific experiment to be a big part of the evolution of a franchise is very unique."

WE'RE OFF TO SEE THE WIZARD

For a franchise savior, the humidor isn't much to look at. It sits off a wide walkway behind the Rockies dugout in the bowels of Coors Field—a 9x9x7.5-foot aluminum box with Styrofoam insulation that looks a lot like a beer cooler.

"It's kind of like the Wizard of Oz," said Kevin Kahn, the club's vice president of stadium operations. "When we show it to people, they say, 'This is it?'"

And it isn't even hiding behind a curtain. Open the padlocked door, step inside on the concrete floor, and there are balls by the dozens in boxes resting on six metal shelves to either side. The capacity is about 4,800 baseballs.

The device includes an electric steam humidifier that maintains a 50-percent humidity reading, and to keep a constant 70-degree temperature, there is a heating and cooling coil. That's why Cowell prefers to call his baby an "environmental chamber" rather than a humidor.

By any name, it has been a monumental game changer at Coors Field. Runs are down. Home runs are way down. Hitters' frustration levels are up, and pitchers are experiencing success where there used to be frustration.

The numbers tell the story: in the pre-humidor days prior to 2002, there were averages of 13.83 runs and 3.20 home runs per game at Coors Field. From 2002-06, the numbers were reduced to 12.25 runs and 2.58 home runs per game. The drop-off was most pronounced in 2006, when only 10.72 runs were scored per game, and home runs fell to 2.07 per game.

By any measure, the Rockies have found a way to level the playing field between hitter and pitcher at their home playing field, and they believe it has changed the course of their future.

"It's given this franchise a chance," O'Dowd said. "I think this ballpark plays better than the place in Philadelphia plays, the place in Texas plays, the place in Cincinnati plays. I still think it's an above-average hitters' park because of the gaps. I think it's a tad above average as a home run park. I still think it's an above-average double and triples ballpark. And I still think you're going to need speed."

If the humidor has heightened the Rockies' chances of building a successful team—and everyone with the franchise believes it has—then it is Hurdle who has benefited doubly. He was the Rockies' hitting instructor before the humidor was installed, and the manager ever since it was put into use.

"We were always battling with the altitude, but on top of that, we were putting into play a smaller, harder ball in our home games," Hurdle said. "Those things were just getting blasted. Now the ball we play with in April is the same size as the one we play with in June, and in September, and there has been a difference in the results.

"We're just trying to make it a level playing ground. It got so tough, we actually thought about trying to develop two different teams—a home team and a road team. People kept thinking out of the box to try to level the playing field, and we just happened to hit on that (humidor)."

Even Cowell, who never played organized baseball, knew the game he was watching at Coors Field in the pre-humidor days wasn't the same one he grew up with at Dodger Stadium. And he didn't like it.

"I wasn't that fond of the product," Cowell said. "Being a fan myself, you get used to seeing what baseball looked like. The game was being played differently in Coors Field than it was everywhere else. I didn't like hearing the comments that were being made. When Todd Helton or Larry Walker had a great year, it was always, 'Yeah, but . . .' There always was a 'Yeah, but . . .'

"We weren't looking to get a competitive advantage. We just wanted to make it so the game was played the way it was everywhere else. It was all for the good of the game. That was the focus."

Even Holliday, the new Bomber, concurs.

"I'd love to take all the balls out of the humidor, but I think it's created a much more competitive atmosphere," he said. "The games are much shorter. It's crisp baseball.

If a guy pitches well, he pitches well. If a guy is making bad pitches, he's going to give it up.

"I don't think hitters have to make as many adjustments going back on the road. Pitchers' pitches here are very similar to the way they are on the road. It's created a more consistent scenario for the offense. Balls that are hit in the air that are supposed to be outs are outs. Balls that are supposed to be homers are homers. The stats show it. The game plays a lot better."

THE BIG SECRET

It took the off-season between the 2001 and 2002 seasons to construct the humidor, and then came the process of getting approval from Major League Baseball and the Players Association. Charlie Monfort explained the experiment to Selig, MLB officials had conversations with Rawlings officials and the players union, and a

Tony Cowell changed the course of franchise history with the development of the humidor.
AP Images

baseball specifications agreement was reached in April of 2002.

Not even the coaching staff and players knew what was going on at first, and the secretive nature of the operation lent to the idea that the Rockies may have been trying to pull a fast one. But club officials say that wasn't the case, and MLB official Jimmie Lee Solomon, chief of the humidor police, confirms this.

"There wasn't any secret about it as far as we were concerned," Solomon said. "They were very clear about what they were doing. We were well aware of it. We didn't have a problem with what they were trying to do, but we said we would monitor it."

Added Kahn: "We told the people we felt we needed to tell. There was the unknown there as far as what might happen, so why speculate if you don't know? We had no set expectations of runs going down by 'X' and home runs going down by 'Y.' So why tell everybody about it?"

And another big event temporarily diverted everyone's attention:

Bell was fired on April 25 and replaced by Hurdle, sparking an immediate turnaround on the field. The Rockies blitzed through a 6-0 homestand during which they allowed two runs or less in five games. It took the reporting of the *Denver Post*'s Mike Klis to remove the cloak on the great humidor experiment.

"Clint probably did heighten the focus and intensity, as changes often do," Klis said. "But he clearly was getting the best pitching in club history—and at Coors Field.

"You could tell with the naked eye that the ball wasn't going anywhere. Balls were getting crushed to center, and Juan Pierre was catching them 20 feet from the warning track.

"So I started poking around and asking questions. I asked 'Chico' (Dan McGinn, the former home clubhouse manager), and he wouldn't say anything. None of the guys knew about it. It was like a secret. One day, Todd Zeile said, 'I know what's going on at Coors Field.' He wouldn't tell me what it was, but he said something was going on.

"Finally, somebody told me they were storing balls in a humidor. I won't ever say who. So I called Keli McGregor and Dan O'Dowd, and Keli, who's real honest and a great guy, took two days to call me back. O'Dowd took a day. Finally they released a statement about it."

CONSPIRACY THEORIES

To this day, the humidor—what it does, and how it does it—remains misunderstood. One American League player, upon his first visit to Coors Field in 2006, mistakenly called it "the humidifier." And when the Rockies advanced to the 2007 World Series, the humidor was a popular tour stop for many who knew little about it.

But it's really quite simple. Pre-2002, the Rockies were using baseballs that weren't within the recommended specifications in terms of weight and circumference.

Out of the Rawlings factory, baseballs weigh from 5 to 5 ¼ ounces and are 9 to 9 ¼ inches around.

But the longer baseballs are stored in the dry Colorado air, the lighter, smaller, harder, and slicker they become. In the pre-humidor days, if you heard it once, you heard it a thousand times from pitchers—they just couldn't get a good grip on the ball.

"So the humidor, as simple a concept as it is, has provided three things," O'Dowd said. "We're now playing with a ball that weight-wise is legitimate, and feels no different grip-wise than any other ball in any other ballpark. And thirdly: mentally, by giving the pitchers something they feel normalizes the game."

But there remains the question: are the Rockies pulling a fast one with ball storage? There is wiggle room, and that creates an integrity issue that lingers in some minds.

Former Rockies infielder Jeff Cirillo speculated in 2006 that the Rockies could use humidor-stored balls when opposing teams are at the plate, and non-stored balls when they are at bat. Nobody takes the anti-humidor stance more strongly than Leyland:

"To be honest with you—I guess I'm going to strike up some controversy here—I'm not sure I agree with it," Leyland said. "I'm not looking for an argument here. But I get kind of a bad feeling about Major League Baseball itself if you're doing something like that.

"If a guy does something (illegal) to the baseball or does something to his bat, they make a big issue out of it. Now we're allowing somebody to do something with the baseball so it doesn't go as far. I'm not sure that should be the way that it is. I'm not saying it hasn't helped. But to me, you're doctoring the baseballs. And that's something you can play with.

"I wouldn't have been in favor of it. I just don't think that's right. I'm not saying people do (tinker with it). I'm not making any accusations. But it is something you can tinker with."

Every so often, results at Coors Field raise eyebrows. Such as the June 18-20, 2002 series against the New York Yankees, when it was as if the Blake Street Bombers reunited. The three final scores were 10-5, 20-10, and 14-11, and the teams combined for 95 hits including 15 home runs. Compare that to the overall averages in that first season of humidor use—12.21 runs and 2.86 homers per game.

Then there was September of 2006, when an average of 16.9 runs per game were scored in 14 games at Coors Field, raising suspicions that the non-humidor-stored balls were in play again, perhaps to prop up record-low offensive production prior to that point.

"There is no tinkering going on," Hurdle reiterated. "What about September (of 2006)? Arms were tired, pitchers made lousy pitches, hitters got hot. It's a combination of things. Plus the humidity does change. And there are days when the ball still flies out of here. It's moreso toward the late part of the season, and it's definitely in day games."

Again Solomon backs the Rockies.

"One can always think something is afoot," he said. "Conspiracy theorists are everywhere. But we are confident nothing is going on. We test balls. They are constantly sending us sample balls. Plus we make unannounced visits. We get there a couple of times a season. If anybody wanted to not follow the rules, they could. But you just trust everybody is doing it properly."

EVERYWHERE A HUMIDOR?

Well, not exactly. But due in part to the lessons learned from the Rockies' experiment, Major League Baseball in 2007 ordered all teams to store baseballs in environmentally controlled areas coming as close as possible to the Rawlings' recommended 70 degrees and 50-percent humidity settings.

"More and more, we see how baseballs could lose moisture, dry out, or be altered by the environment in some way," Solomon said. "Basically, we want to keep all baseballs as close to manufacturer-suggested environmental levels as long as possible.

"And we've told teams not to use balls from the previous year for games, only for batting practice. They could be subject to a number of things, sitting around that long. Up until the Rockies, we didn't monitor it closely. They made us give more scrutiny to this issue. I think the Rockies were ahead of their time."

If imitation is the sincerest form of flattery, consider Cowell surprised and grateful.

"I had no idea it would take off and get big like it has," Cowell said. "Personally, it's gratifying that I was able to help baseball, help the fans, the team, the players."

There has been no letter of commendation to Cowell from Selig for changing the game at altitude and starting a baseball-storage revolution. But compliments from players and coaches have been nice to hear.

"Don Baylor told me, 'I wish I had that (humidor) when I was here,'" Cowell said. "'Why didn't you come up with it back then? I might still be here.'"

THEN AND NOW

There really is only one hitter who can best describe the difference between pre-humidor Coors Field and the current conditions. But if you think he's going to rail on about what could have been, or how things are unfair to hitters now, you don't know Helton very well.

"It's better for the team; it's better for the game," Helton said. "It's definitely a better game. When you hit a ball in the gap, outfielders are able to run them down, whereas in the past, they wouldn't be able to run them down. That's the biggest difference I notice. And I think (the humidor) makes a bigger difference when the weather is cool.

"I don't feel cheated. I'd rather win. Everybody wants to have a good year and put up good numbers, but some years you don't. There are a lot of factors that can go into that. The humidor is definitely one of those factors. It's a big factor, but it's not the huge, deciding factor. It can also be used as an excuse. It's human nature; when something goes wrong, you find an excuse."

This leads to the debate about the talent on the field through 13 years of games at Coors Field. Do the Rockies simply have better pitchers now than they used to? How would the Blake Street Bombers fare under the current conditions? Would Holliday have been just as potent as the old Bombers if he were playing under pre-humidor conditions?

"It would be interesting to see, with all the big money we spent on pitching, what would have happened if the humidor would have been in effect back then," McMorris said. "How much difference it could have made, we'll never know."

We'll never know for certain, but there is no shortage of opinions. The gamut runs from Klis to Jason Jennings, with Hurdle in the middle.

"People who don't think the humidor has much impact forget what it was like before," Klis said. "It's not the pitching. I can't say this enough. What is going on at Coors Field now has nothing to do with better pitching. There's no way Jason Jennings is better than Bill Swift.

"Jeff Francis? He'll be lucky to match Denny Neagle's career stats. Denny Neagle had a 20-4 year. He averaged 15 wins over seven straight years. Is Jeff Francis going to average 15 wins over the next seven years? With the humidor, he's got a shot. But before the humidor, I'm telling you, he had no chance. No one did."

Jennings, the winningest pitcher in franchise history, won the National League Rookie of the Year Award with a 16-8 record in 2002, the first year of humidor use. Over five-plus seasons, nobody was more durable and successful at Coors Field.

By 2006, when complaints about the humidor increased in direct correlation with the record-low offense being produced at the park, Jennings had heard enough. He spoke out for himself and his fellow pitching brethren.

"Everybody was griping about the humidor—it was doing this and that to the ball,'" Jennings said. "But we were pitching pretty well. I think (the drop in runs) had at least something to do with how we were throwing the ball. There are better pitchers there now.

"It's a little different, but it's still a hitters' park. And I've said all along that it's not so much the home runs. It's the bloopers, the doubles in the gaps that turn into triples, and everybody taking that extra base."

Says Hurdle, who has seen it all: "I think the Bombers' numbers today would be close to what they were. You can't cut them in half. Those guys were legit. I don't want people to take away from the talent those guys had.

"The same is true for the pitchers today. They have made better pitches. They have kept the ball down. When pitchers have success, it rings true every year—they keep it down, keep it away or tight, work the corners. When they get it up over the plate and elevate it, they get splattered.

"Holliday (as a pre-humidor hitter)? He hit 34 (homers in 2006). I don't think there would be any doubt that he would have hit 40 with no humidor."

10

COMIC RELIEF

When it came to the Rockies bullpen and its inhabitants back in the early days, Gebhard says he preferred to keep it on a don't-need-to-know basis.

"Just as long as the relievers came in and got it done, I didn't need to know about what else was going on down there," he said.

Considering Gebhard had his hand in virtually everything else connected with operating the franchise, that's quite a statement. Then again, maybe that was a good thing. But now that the statute of limitations has expired on the wacky activities of Rockies relievers of yesteryear, Gebhard will hear the truth. Well, some of it, anyway.

Dipoto wore many hats in his days with the Rockies: setup man, closer, front office executive, broadcaster, baseball historian, and memorabilia collector. And now, he takes on the task of bullpen tour guide.

BLOCKS OF WISDOM

"There was a room in the back of the bullpen (at Coors Field) where the grounds crew stored some of their stuff. It was like a little hideout back there, and the wall was made of cinder blocks—painted blocks with a shiny finish.

"The year before I got there, the guys started a tradition where each of them took a block and wrote a message. It was going to be a thing where sooner or later every block on the wall would have a message from somebody who had been there. The only rule was: you weren't allowed to get your block until you experienced giving up four runs in an inning, because it was a given that it was going to happen to everybody.

"Mine came when I was pitching against the Mets for the first time after they traded me to the Rockies. I was probably as nervous as I ever was in a big-league game, pitching against guys who had been my teammates. I didn't get an out, gave up four runs, and walked off.

"Steve Reed walks up, rubs me on the hair and says, 'OK, you can have your brick now.' My message was something like, 'It's like playing in a pinball machine. You never know what you're going to see. But hold on tight, there's no better place to play in baseball.'

"For the longest time, we got all over (Mike) DeJean because when he first got to the big leagues, his first 25 innings or so, he was lights out. So he wasn't allowed to have a block. But then finally he got his too. It's all been painted over, and that disappoints me. There had to have been 20 blocks, all with different messages."

THE WWF

"That back room . . . it got a little wild in there some games. We would actually take the replacement pads they had for the outfield wall, and we'd line the room with them, and have steel-cage wrestling matches. Guys would be throwing each other around off the pads, tagging in and out. We'd spend a couple innings just trying to distract ourselves because once the fifth inning cleared, we were like a fire company. It was time to answer the bell.

"The most psychotic with it were Darren Holmes and Mike Munoz. They were fanatical. Holmie thought he was Ric Flair. He had all these moves, and the whole time he was chirping at you. It was right around the time when Creatine was the supplement everybody was using, and Holmie would say, 'I took my Creatine today. Wait 'till you see this.' Next thing you know, you were getting thrown up against a brick wall."

THE DUMMY

"There was a dummy down there, in the room in the back. It was kind of like a CPR-Annie dummy—it sat in the corner, and it never left. Nobody ever knew why it was there; it was just there. And it essentially served as a punching bag. It had no name, but it had all kinds of stuff over it.

"We'd come out and put Band-Aids on it where somebody had beaten it the night before. It wasn't solely for the relievers, either. Walker took advantage of it as much as anybody. He'd walk back there after making an out in a big situation—one of the rare times he did—and he'd shut the door to the back room, and you'd hear the dummy just getting its butt kicked."

EMOTIONAL RESCUE

"Steve Reed was usually the loudest guy in the group, but he didn't wake up in a game until about the sixth inning. He'd lay low for four or five innings, and then he'd come alive because he knew that was our time.

"His big thing was the stat sheet. He'd grab it, bark out the numbers, and start this rant: 'What have we got? Curtis (Leskanic)? Rick Wilkins? Can I tell the women and children to hide? 0-for-16 with 13 punchouts? How is that humanly possible?'

"He'd go through the whole list like that. When we played the Padres, it was Ruffin and Tony Gwynn. Ruff had a lot of success with Tony Gwynn. Who has success with Tony Gwynn? But Ruff did. Reeder would bark out the numbers and say, 'You know who you're going to be facing tonight.' What he was doing was building up guys' confidence. He wanted you to be aggressive.

"He was great for the team, great for chemistry. Relief pitchers aren't usually the backbone or the leaders of the team, but Reeder had a lot of leadership qualities. And he had guts. I don't know if I ever played with anybody who had more guts than Steve Reed. He didn't care what the situation was, what the time was. He threw every day, never turned down the ball."

A HALLMARK MOMENT

It's not difficult for Dipoto to recall his low moment with the Rockies. It came in the final week of the 1997 season, when the team was on the verge of being eliminated, and in a game in Florida he gave up a walkoff grand slam to Bobby Bonilla. But there was one consolation:

"We had a one-run lead, I got into a jam and gave up the grand slam," Dipoto said. "It was an epic at-bat, 12 pitches, and he's fouling off pitches left and right. That game pretty much killed our playoff hopes. After that game we got on the plane, and I was beside myself. That was about the most disappointing thing you could do.

"Jason Bates was sitting a seat over from me. He was trying to get my mind off it. Then John Burke came over, too. He was, very quietly, one of the funniest guys on the team. He had a greeting card from his wife that he had carried with him all year long.

"The card said something like, 'John, hang in there, I know you've got it in you.' It was a really nice sentimental message because he had gone through a lot with injuries. So he carried this card, and everywhere we went, he put it up in his locker.

"So at one point during the flight, Burkie hands me the card, and I said, 'Dude, what are you doing?'

"And he says, 'You need it, man, you need it.'

"I opened up the card, and where it said, 'John' he had crossed it out and written, 'Jerry.' And where it said, 'I love you, Liz' he had crossed it out and written, 'I like you a lot, John.' I kept that card with me for the rest of my career."

MARATHON MAN

Even in a bullpen full of characters, Leskanic stood out. Most of the time, he just couldn't help himself. But on occasion, there was a method to his madness.

"We were going through a rough period in 1997," Dipoto said. "We had just gone into Texas and San Francisco and got crushed. I mean, this was a bad road trip. So, first day back in Denver, everybody gets to

Jerry Dipoto wore many hats in his Rockies' days, including setup man, closer, and member of the front office. *AP Images*

the clubhouse around 2-2:30 in the afternoon, and Curtis had pulled the treadmill out of the weight room and into the clubhouse.

"He's right there when you walk in. You couldn't miss him. And he's wearing his Pittsburgh Steelers helmet, tennis shoes, and that's it. And he's running about 100 mph on the treadmill. I don't know how long he ran, but it was for quite a while, because he waited for every guy to walk in.

"And when you walked in, you dropped all the heaviness, all the weight of the bad trip. You couldn't help but laugh. It was fabulous. It got everybody to forget the miserable trip. We were back to doing what we usually do. We were having fun again."

SING A LITTLE SONG FOR ME

Major league players are notoriously superstitious, and the Rockies were no exception. Walker's obsession with the number three was legendary, and Leskanic had his own routine filled with idiosyncrasies.

Whenever the call came for him to begin warming up, he had to put his head in the sink and drench his hair with water and shake it out. Then he would swing a heavy metal ball, and do one more thing . . .

"When Curtis would come into a game, sometimes he'd ask me to sing something for him," Weiss said. "He'd throw a couple of balls, step off the mound, and call me in from shortstop. He'd say, 'Sing me a song, man.'

"I'd say, 'What do you want?'

"He'd throw out a song or a singer, and I'd have to sing it to him. He'd kind of nod, and go, 'All right.' Pearl Jam, Springsteen, anybody. I'd have to sing a couple of bars. He might sing a couple words back."

And what happened after Weiss left the team in 1998?

"Curtis would leave the pen, and before he'd go, he needed a song from one of us, something to keep him loose," Dipoto said. "One day I remember, we're getting shellacked, he's dead tired, his arm is ready to fall off, and he looks over to us in the bullpen.

"I said, 'Lesky, what song do you need?'

"And he said, '"Dead Man Walking."'

"Usually, he would take a couple of hops and then run to the mound. But this time, he turned around and walked in like Lee Smith. I mean he walked in really, really slow."

MAYNE ON THE MOUND

Bell has been in the game his entire adult life—40 years as a player, coach, manager and front office executive—and he says the night of August 22, 2000 "might have been the most memorable game I've ever been a part of."

It went in the books as a 7-6 Rockies win over the Braves in 12 innings, but a check of the box score reveals what Bell is talking about. At the bottom of a long list of Rockies pitchers—10, to be exact—is this line: Mayne WP 1 1 0 1 0.

Yes, catcher Brent Mayne took the mound in the top of the 12th inning—unbeknownst to Bell—for the first time in his entire life. And not only did Mayne go through the top of the Braves' lineup without allowing a run, but he did something no position player had done since Rocky Colavito 32 years earlier.

When Adam Melhuse delivered his first major-league hit and RBI in the bottom of the 12th, Mayne became the game's winning pitcher. Jeff Kingery's call on KOA summed it up rather nicely: "If you didn't watch it, if you didn't listen to it, you wouldn't believe it."

And to think, it all started when the usually mild-mannered Galarraga, by then a Brave, charged the mound after being hit by a John Wasdin pitch in the top of the 11th, setting off a bench-clearing incident.

After Wasdin and Bell were ejected, Brian Bohanon, who had thrown six innings and 99 pitches the previous night, had to get the final out in the 11th inning. Bell had already blown through the entire seven-man bullpen after starter Masato Yoshii went only 5⅓ innings.

Bell was back in his office, pondering what to do next—Astacio was pleading to go in the game, Pierre was a position-player possibility—when Mayne, who wasn't playing due to a wrist injury, happened to walk by.

"We had just had the brawl, so I went back downstairs to watch the video," Mayne said. "I wanted to see if anybody got smoked or whatever, to see the little things you don't see when you're in the fight.

"I went by the first (office) door, and then before the second door, (Bell) popped out in front of me, looking kind of frantic. He said, 'Come in here a minute, I want to talk to you. What am I going to do right here? Who can pitch? Do you think Juan (Pierre) can pitch?'

"And I said, 'Yeah, I think Juan can pitch. He's the youngest guy. He can take the ball.'"

Then Bell asked the fateful question to Mayne: "Can you pitch?"

"He said, 'Yeah, I can pitch,'" Bell recalled. "And I said, 'All right, you're in.' I found out later he had never pitched—ever. I don't think there was one player in that clubhouse who had never pitched, except for Brent Mayne. So, smart guy that I am, I sent Brent Mayne out there. It wasn't a very intelligent decision."

But as it turned out, it was a historical one. Mayne's cap and a ball from the game are in the Hall of Fame to prove it.

"I threw 15-20 balls in the cage, went into the dugout, sat next to Ben (Petrick), and said, 'One's a fastball, two's a curve . . .'" Mayne said.

"And Ben says, 'What are you talking about?'

"I said, 'I'm going in to pitch.' As a catcher, you're always looking out toward the outfield. You don't feel the fans much. But when you turn it around and you're looking (from the mound), you say, 'Damn, there are a lot of people here.'"

The first batter Mayne faced was Glavine, who was pinch-hitting for a reliever. Glavine bounced back to Mayne, and Weiss—another Rockie-turned-Brave at that point—flew out to center on the first pitch. Two outs, nobody on. Piece of cake, right? Well, not exactly.

Rafael Furcal blistered a hard shot right through Mayne's legs—a drive that left Mayne hunched over like a long-snapper, watching through his legs as the ball skipped into center field for a single.

"Then it kind of struck home—this was for real," Mayne said.

And up stepped Andruw Jones.

"Andruw? I wanted no part of that. Now I was scared," Mayne said. "I just wanted to get the last out, just survive it. I walked him. Then Chipper (Jones)—same feeling."

But Chipper, who would win the National League MVP that season, was retired on a harmless excuse-me-swing groundout to third. And then it was time for Melhuse to make history—his own, and for Mayne.

"In all the years I played, that was the most attention I had gotten," Mayne said. "It was a pretty odd moment."

THE MANIC MOODS OF MARVIN FREEMAN

Marvin Freeman. For those who were around him, it's hard to hide a smirk when his name rolls off your tongue.

Marvin Freeman, right, and Jeff Reed question umpire Rick Rieker's call during a 1996 game. *AP Images*

He was one of the best bargain signings of the Rockies' early years, and then he became one of their worst signings. Gebhard snagged him for $500,000 in the winter of 1993, and Freeman was the best starter on the 1994 squad, going 10-2 with a sparkling 2.80 ERA in the strike-shortened season.

That earned Freeman a two-year, $4.4-million deal, but he didn't live up to it. There were injury problems, but really he lost the support of management and teammates with moodiness and selfish behavior. Midway through the 1996 season, he was released after going 10-16 with a 6.04 ERA after signing the two-year deal.

At 6-7, it was hard to miss him, especially when it was a travel day and he was dressed to the nines. Most of the time you couldn't help but hear him, either. But on days he pitched, if you happened to venture into the clubhouse during batting practice, you would see a figure on a couch, totally covered in white towels, with a little peephole around his face, puffing on a cigarette. That was Marvin, too.

And for all his imitation "gangsta" behavior in the clubhouse, he really did work as a craftsman for a violin bow-making company as a teenager. A walking bunch of contrasts is what he was.

Siegle speaks for the many who remember Freeman mostly with disdain:

"The day he was released, it was me, Geb, Don, and the pitching coach—we all brought him in to release him," Siegle said. "I think everybody really enjoyed it. There aren't many releases you enjoy, but that was one of them. And after he left, there was a standing ovation in the clubhouse."

That left Bailey in the minority. For some reason still inexplicable to him, Bailey got to know a different side of Freeman.

"I loved Marvin," Bailey said. "He wanted to be the hard-ass guy from the ghetto. That's how he wanted to come across. But I remember one day in spring training in 1995, he's having a cigarette, talking away like he usually did. But he pulls me to the side, and says, 'Where are your investments?'

"I said, 'What are you talking about?'

"And he pulls out the *Wall Street Journal* and says, 'I want to show you, because you might make some money in this game. I want you to understand the market.'

"He watched his money. He was sneaky intelligent. But as soon as somebody came around the corner, he was not going to let his guard down. He became 'Snoop Dog' again."

TOO COOL FOR SCHOOL?

The three World Series rings and a National League Manager of the Year Award were still in his future, but in the first three years of the Rockies' existence, Joe Girardi already had established his reputation as a leader and tactician.

Ask teammates about him, and this is what you hear: "He was managing while he was playing." "He was the backbone." "His leadership was his biggest asset." And Girardi was smart, too—engineering-degree-from-Northwestern-University smart. In fact, when the Rockies made an early trip to Dodger Stadium one season, the scoreboard noted as much.

"We go into Dodger Stadium, and they put up on the scoreboard that he was a two-time academic All-American at Northwestern," Baylor said. "So later that year, we're in Philly, and they've got the bases loaded and (Darren) Daulton is coming up. I go to the mound—I think Ruffin was pitching—and Joe says, 'What are we going to do, Skip?'

"And that's when I said, 'You're the two-time academic All-American; you figure it out.' And then I left the mound. You know, to lighten the mood a little bit. Take the pressure off. What were you going to do? If it was Ruffin, you were going to slider (Daulton) to death."

THE CREATURE

Marriages don't last this long; careers have shorter life spans—but for eight years of his 14-year major league career—including all four with the Rockies—Weiss played shortstop using one glove, and one glove only. "The Creature" is what former A's teammate Mike Bordick named it. He wouldn't even touch the thing, it was so beat up and defaced.

It was a Mizuno with a model number Weiss can no longer remember. And by the time Weiss finally had to retire it, the glove bore little resemblance to the one that came from the factory. Broken-in was one thing, but this glove had been just plain broken so many times that it was a wonder it could be fixed. It had been sewed and stitched, even held together at times by fishing line.

"It probably had 20 different surgeries," Weiss said. "I got it in 1992. I wasn't planning on using it for as long as I did. But it was one of those things where I was terrible at breaking in gloves, and this one, for whatever reason, I got just right, and once I started using it for one year, then another, then another, anything else I put on my hand felt foreign to me.

"So I was a slave to it after a while. As much as it broke down later in my career, I couldn't use anything else. It was too late. It just molded to my hand."

Speaking of breakdowns . . .

"One time at Coors Field, I caught a line drive, and it blew out the strings that kept the fingers together. It just blew out two fingers. That was the first out of the inning, so I played the rest of the inning like that. If the ball had come to me, it would have gone right through my glove. But I didn't get any more balls that inning."

Another blowout came at an absolutely critical time.

"I'm with the Braves, we're playing in the World Series against the Yankees (in 1999), and I'm playing catch with Chipper Jones in front of the dugout. It's real close to game time, and the umpires are out on the field. Chipper throws the ball to me, and the glove just literally explodes. The thumb tore away from the rest of the glove.

"I hadn't used anything else in eight years. I ran over and threw it to our trainer Jeff Porter. I said, 'Do what you can.' He knew how attached I was to this glove, and he was one of those glove geniuses. He could fix anything. Luckily, we were playing on the road in Yankee Stadium, so I didn't have to go out on the field first. He took leather string and just reattached the thumb, and wrapped the string around the rest of the glove. If you saw it, you would say, 'No way am I using that in a game.'

"But I ended up using it the whole World Series. I don't think I made any errors, but the whole time I was thinking, 'If he hits me the ball, what's going to happen here?' I got through it, but that was the end of the glove. It was eight years old, but it looked like it was 20."

THE VOICE

When Alan Roach resigned from his job as the only public address announcer in club history after 14 seasons, he left big shoes to fill. Or should we say pipes? Just as much as inflated scores and late-inning comebacks, Roach's booming voice was part of the experience of attending Rockies home games.

The drawn-out "Laaarrrryyy" in "Larry Walker" and the rapid-fire "BradHawpe" were two signature calls from the deepest bass you've ever heard. But it's not that difficult to guess Roach's two favorite names to announce, especially when you know that on the audition tape he made in 1992—even before the expansion draft—two players he included were Galarraga and Bichette.

"Syllable-wise, the best name to say was Andres Galarraga," said Roach, who left the position to spend more time with his two young children. "But my favorite was Dante Bichette because of what it meant for me to say it.

"I grew up in Minnesota, and every game I ever went to, (the late) Bob Casey did the PA. I loved how he announced Kirby Puckett's name, and I announced Dante's name the same way. After I got the job, I wrote to Bob, and we ended up being good friends, and I miss him a lot."

But there is one player announcement Roach would rather forget.

"The Rockies were playing the Cubs, and that same night Mark McGwire got traded to the Cardinals," Roach said. "So that was the buzz around the ballpark. All night, everybody was talking about Mark McGwire.

"So we get to the start of an inning, and I say, 'Leading off for the Cubs, first baseman, No. 17, Mark McGwire'. But it was Mark Grace. I talked to Grace about it later, and he remembered it. He said he grounded out to second base, went back to the dugout, and said, 'What the hell did he call me?'"

GENERATION "R"

STARTING OVER AGAIN

After the initial burst that coincided with Hurdle replacing Bell, the 2002 Rockies turned out to be no different than the 2001 version. The 6-0 start under Hurdle built to an impressive 24-10 stretch through June 1, but second-half losing streaks of eight games, nine games, and five games to end the season left the Rockies at 73-89 again. At least they didn't finish last—they moved up a spot to fourth.

The 2003 season was almost another duplicate. The Rockies finished fourth again, and improved by only one game, making it 74-88. The ineptitude deepened in 2004, when nine losses in their last 10 games left the Rockies with a 68-94 record. But a critically important decision was made during the course of that season, one that eventually would pay huge dividends and prove to be a turning point in the organization's history. And that involved the R word—as in rebuilding.

"It started in '01, '02, and '03, but the full-blown commitment came in '04," O'Dowd said. "We didn't have the players to do it in '01, '02, '03. Just because you say you want to build from within doesn't mean you have the type of players to do it. It wasn't until '04 that Dick and Charlie made the commitment that they were going to own the club for a long time, and this is the kind of organization model we were going to follow."

The problem was that one losing season after another alienated what had been arguably the game's best fan base. Season home attendance dipped below three million for the first time in 2002, and below two million for the only time in franchise history in 2005, corresponding with the lowest win total (67) since 1993. And like during O'Dowd's early years in charge, a patch-quilt roster remained the only constant while the Generation R core group of young players established themselves.

Only Charles Johnson (2003-04) had more than a one-year run as the regular catcher, with Mayne, Petrick, Gary Bennett, Danny Ardoin, and J. D. Closser in the long line that came before the Torrealba/Chris Iannetta pairing in 2007.

Before Matsui's bounce-back 2007 season, second base was a revolving door of platoon combinations—Todd Walker and Jose Ortiz, Ortiz and Brent Butler, Aaron Miles and Luis Gonzalez—with a year each from Ronnie Belliard and Jamey Carroll mixed in.

Between Perez's departure and Tulowitzki's arrival, Juan Uribe, Jose Hernandez, Royce Clayton, and Clint Barmes all had opportunities at shortstop.

There was a different third baseman every year from 2001-04, with Cirillo, Zeile, Chris Stynes, and Castilla preceding Atkins.

Between Bichette and Holliday, left fielders included Bragg, Ron Gant, Ochoa, Todd Hollandsworth, and Jay Payton.

The long list of center fielders prior to Taveras included Hamilton, Goodwin, Pierre, Preston Wilson, Jeromy Burnitz, and Cory Sullivan. Burnitz also logged a season in right field as the bridge between Walker and Hawpe.

But by 2007, the new Rockies surrounded the lone mainstay, Helton. And finally, a new and winning identity was established.

"We didn't feel good about what we were doing until we made the commitment in '04 to do things the way we are doing them now," O'Dowd said. "Once we did that, we felt great about our future.

"For the first time, we were all on the same page from top down. There was no backing up, there was no running away from it. We were going to create opportunities for our young players."

As hitting instructor and manager, Clint Hurdle has worn a Rockies uniform since 1997.
AP Images

THE FACE OF THE FRANCHISE

Hurdle was particularly entertaining during the Rockies' unexpected month-long romp to the pennant and World Series, filling media notebooks and providing high-quality sound bites on a daily basis. Those who were around him for the first time couldn't help but be impressed, learning that a clutch performer "has a slow heartbeat," and a pitcher who can get out of jams "works well in traffic." Hurdle also openly discussed everything from the humidor, to the ups and downs of a life in baseball, to the blessings of raising a five-year-old daughter born with a rare genetic defect.

And on the eve of World Series Game 1, he took the time to explain the touching significance of why he wrote the number 64 on each game's lineup card—in memory of Kyle Blakeman, a teenage football player who died of cancer two months earlier, shortly after a couple of hospital visits from Hurdle and his wife.

Yes, Hurdle was front and center again, the lead voice for a team on a historic roll, which had its own happy irony.

The rebuilding program that coincided with Hurdle's ascension from hitting instructor to manager in late April 2002 came complete with growing pains. As the consecutive-losing-seasons streak grew to six in 2006, so did criticism of the organization—aimed mostly at the top—and even worse, apathy.

But you could always count on Hurdle to put a positive spin on the proceedings, to be a human shield of positivism and patience, protecting his bosses and players alike.

Alves recalls one particularly down moment during the club's lean years, and how Hurdle lightened it.

"We were in Tampa Bay, and we had lost three games there, after losing three to the Yankees," Alves said. "On the play that lost the last game, Choo Freeman was playing center, and he got disoriented going after a ball. He picked it up and threw it into the left-field corner.

"So we lose the game, get on the bus to go to the airport, and it's pouring. We get off the bus and get on the plane, and the storm is right over us. It's hailing. You could hear the hail hitting the plane. Then the pilot comes on and says, 'Sorry guys, we're going to be here a bit.' And Clint turns around and yells, 'Stay hot, Rockies.' It just broke the tension. It was hilarious. That was a good moment.

"He took on an incredible role—spokesman for the club—at a very difficult time under a lot of pressure, and he handled it with a lot of diplomacy and class."

Then all of a sudden, his Rockies team grew up around him in 2007, and Hurdle temporarily moved to the background. When the Rockies got good, Hurdle went low-profile and let his players play and carry more of the load. During the NLCS, Holliday spoke about the changes in his manager.

"When I was a first- or second-year player, we had a lot of first- and second-year players," he said. "As we've gotten older, and gotten a bit more experience, he's let us go out and play, and just kind of sits back and makes the moves he needs to make. I think he has done a great job of transforming."

But on the biggest stage, there was Hurdle again—manager, media-savvy point man, storyteller, and life coach—and loving every minute of it. Asked about the progression of then-to-now for himself and his team, Hurdle needed multiple paragraphs to capture his emotions:

"It's one of those things I hold near and dear to my heart," he said. "I really believe we're prepared for the future through our past. I really believe if we listen and we watch, we can learn. Patience has become a very important tool for me, and it's not one that's easily learned.

"Also, the importance of keeping humility in your back pocket is one of the best things I was ever told as a young player that I never understood until I was an older player. There are two kinds of people who play this game—those who are humble and those who are about to be. At the age of 18, I laughed, said, 'Yeah, that's cute.' Well, by the age of 38, I was wearing it.

"This is something that has a lot of meaning to me, the fact that it has become something that is very, very special, that has given our organization value, that has brought joy to a lot of different people on many different levels."

THE NEW BOMBER

Holliday's hotel-room phone rang early on the Monday morning before the 2007 All-Star Game, and after a couple of rings, he answered. Sort of. Alves recalls the conversation:

"I called Matt in his room, and I said, 'Matt, Jay Alves here.' And he said, 'Huh?' He was still half-asleep.

"And I said, 'I was just asked by people from Major League Baseball if you'd want to be in the home-run hitting contest tonight. They need a replacement for Miguel Cabrera. He just dropped out.' And he said, 'Huh? I don't know.'

"I had just finished pumping him up for 10 minutes to the MLB people, saying he'd be great. So I said, 'Matt, I told them you'd love to participate. I need to get back to them with an answer pretty quickly.'

"So he said he would call me back, and within five, 10 minutes, he called, all awake by now, and said, 'I'd love to do that.'"

And for much of the casual American baseball-watching public, Holliday's performance later that night served as a belated coming-out party for one of the game's best sluggers.

Around the National League, Holliday's power was already no secret. In fact, at 6-foot-4 and 230 pounds of solid muscle, Holliday possesses the kind of power that prompts O'Dowd to say with admiration, "Athletically, he's a freak. He is blessed with some of the most dynamic physical strength of any player I've ever been around. Better than Albert Belle, who also was a freak."

And it's not just Holliday's power, but his ability to win a batting title that made him one of the most dangerous hitters in the National League over the 2006-07 seasons. But after that cool night at AT&T Park, every fan watching had to know it, too.

Belting pitches thrown by his brother Josh, Holliday advanced to the semifinal round of the competition, where he was defeated by Toronto's Alex Rios. One of Holliday's blasts went 475 feet—the second-longest of the entire night.

More than the power display, it was the camera time Holliday received between rounds, when he sat with four-year-old son Jackson in his lap—a slice of Americana if there ever was one—that won hearts for the Rockies' new Bomber.

Typical of his low-key personality, two months after that event, Holliday said he hadn't watched the tape of it yet. He also said, "I'd never do anything just to receive national attention. I did it because I thought it would be a cool experience, and to have my brother be involved in it. It was something I thought would be a neat to have on my baseball resume."

But there was no downplaying the night's importance in the minds of Rockies officials.

"You could look and say, 'He's a Rockie; he's one of our guys,'" Alves said. "He's a star. That's what had been building here. It was a treat. It has been so fun watching Matt grow into what he's become."

And like the Rockies' long, slow climb back to respectability,

Matt Holliday holds his NLCS MVP trophy after the Rockies' sweep of Arizona. *AP Images*

Holliday's success wasn't easy in coming. His size, strength, and power are no surprise considering he comes from a very athletic family. His father Tom is associate head baseball coach at North Carolina State after a stay at Oklahoma State. His uncle Dave is one of O'Dowd's special assistants. Brother Josh is the hitting instructor at Arizona State University. And in fact, Holliday was recruited out of Stillwater High to play quarterback at Oklahoma State, but instead chose to sign with the Rockies, fulfilling his childhood dream to be a pro baseball player.

But despite the power, Holliday's highest home-run total in the Minors was 16 at A-ball in 1999. In his last minor-league season, he hit only 12 in 522 at-bats at Double-A Tulsa.

"I've always been blessed with strength. I've always had power," Holliday said. "But there is a difference between having power and being able to use it. Through the Minors, with a lot of trial, I figured out how to use it better. How to use my balance and my swing, and take advantage of the power I've been blessed with."

As it turned out, Holliday's All-Star adventure was a springboard to bigger things in the Rockies' run to the World Series. He would hit .340 to win the batting title, drive in 137 runs to win the RBI title, and also total 36 home runs, 216 hits, and 120 runs scored. During a two-week September hot streak, he hit .396 with 11 homers and 21 RBIs, and his head-first slide to score the winning run in the play-in game was the stuff of legends.

Alas, all of that wasn't quite enough for Holliday to join Walker as the club's only National League MVPs, finishing a close second to Jimmy Rollins. But at least now everybody knows there is a new Bomber in town.

COOKING WITH A DOSE OF REALITY

For a guy who makes his living throwing a power sinking fastball, Aaron Cook sure has lifted more than his share of spirits. His is a comeback victory in the game of life, not just between the lines.

Holliday is the MVP candidate. Francis has emerged as the staff ace. Tulowitzki captured fans in droves during his run at a National League Rookie of the Year Award that should have been his. But the soul of the Generation R Rockies is a freckle-faced redhead who brushed with death and lives to tell about it.

The night of August 7, 2004, when Cook left the mound feeling dizzy and short of breath and ended up in Rose Medical Center, where blood clots were discovered in his lung, is three-plus years in the rearview mirror. He has won 24 big-league games, started a World Series game, and signed a $30-million contract extension since then. But the three huge scars he sees on his chest every day are all the reminders Cook needs to stay grounded and grateful.

"That night, the doctor and paramedic looked at me and said, 'We don't know how you're alive right now,'" Cook said. "At any time, one of the clots could have broken off and lodged in my heart, or in my brain. Basically, I was a walking time bomb.

"I never did lose consciousness. When I got to the hospital, it was a really surreal feeling. My wife and son were by my bedside the whole time, and when the doctor told us what it was, we just cried for about an hour, realizing the potential of what could have been."

The quick thinking of Rockies trainers Tom Probst and Keith Dugger, who made the decision to get Cook to the hospital immediately, may have saved his life.

"At that moment, I wasn't really sure whether or not I would play baseball again, and it really didn't matter," Cook said. "It made me realize that baseball wasn't the most important thing in my life. My friends and family are. It's really put things in perspective."

Still, the competitor in Cook told the attending physician, "I have to pitch again in five days, so hurry up and get me better." However, a long recovery process awaited, including two surgeries—the first an eight-hour procedure in which a rib was removed on Cook's right side to relieve compression on a vein. The second surgery helped return his blood flow to normal, and 11 months later Cook was back in the Majors with another mission besides pitching.

"My faith has played a big part in my recovery," he said. "I put my trust in God, that He had everything under control, and that I was still alive for a reason. Through the whole ordeal, I've had a great opportunity to share my story—what God has meant to me, and where perseverance has gotten me.

"I believe everything that's in the Bible, but sometimes when you relate your personal story, it comes across in a different light. I'm taking the opportunity to share what I've been through. With God's help, I was able to overcome it."

Slowly, word is spreading beyond Colorado. The Boston chapter of the Baseball Writers Association of America awarded Cook the Tony Conigliaro Award in 2006, presented annually to a player who has overcome adversity.

Cook made one more impressive comeback last season with a strong showing in Game 4 of the World Series after missing two-and-a-half months with a strained oblique muscle—which, after all he had been through, should have surprised nobody.

"If I hadn't been able to come back, I think I could have walked away from the game pretty easily," Cook said. "But I think it refocused my career. Once baseball had been taken away for awhile, I started to enjoy it a little bit more when I got back. I started to have more fun when I came to the ballpark. I'm not the guy who puts my headphones on and sits in front of my locker. I try to have fun with my teammates.

"I was gone for almost a full year before I made it back to the big leagues. For a while there, I couldn't even throw a baseball 30 feet. So to be able to go through that rehab and be back in the position I'm in, I'm thankful."

SO NOW WHAT?

The success of 2007 will enable the payroll to be increased by more than 20 percent for 2008, but one thing that isn't going to change is the Rockies' organizational approach.

"In getting through those difficult times, I think we saved the franchise, because we have an organization that now has a clear vision of what we need to be," O'Dowd said. "Which is an organization built around scouting and development of its own players. I think we're close to having a pretty good run here. I believe we are positioned really well right now.

"We may not be able to hold on to all of these guys, but we'll hold on to some of them. In Cleveland, we lost (Albert) Belle, we lost (Kenny) Lofton, we lost (Jim) Thome, we lost (Manny) Ramirez, and we continued to win. You have to know who you are, and you have to know when to move players, and you have to constantly be able to develop players to replace the ones you lose. That's what we're going to be."

This does-he-stay-or-does-he-go question arose following the 2006 season with Jennings, and the Rockies acted decisively—and as it turned out, profitably. When their three-year contract offer fell far short of Jennings' expectations, they decided to trade him to the Astros rather than have him enter a final season in Colorado before free agency. In return, the Rockies got three productive players in Taveras, Hirsh, and Buchholz.

"We were offered something we liked, so we decided to do it at that point," O'Dowd said.

Jennings had no hard feelings, but also questioned the organization's financial ability to commit to its core players.

"It was the best they could do; I understood that," Jennings said. "They were working with the budget they had, and the market took off with Gil Meche and Ted Lilly. I had to do what was best for me. The Rockies did what was best for them. No regrets. It was just a business decision.

Coming off their first pennant, the Rockies addressed the business of keeping their core players in place by giving out three significant contracts extensions over the winter. Cook received a three-year, $30-million deal that will extend through what could have been two years of free agency.

Holliday signed a two-year, $23-million deal that will take him through his fifth and sixth seasons, and he remains open to the possibility of staying longer even though he could be looking at a deal work well over $100 million if he opts for free agency after the 2009 season.

"Any time you get a chance to play with your friends, guys you've known five, six, seven years, these are relationships that are special," Holliday said. "I've watched a lot of them grow from minor-leaguers to the players they are today. When you see guys who you deeply care for get better and make strides, you're genuinely happy for them and excited for what they've become.

"It's been pretty exciting, a pleasure to watch. I'd love to be able to keep playing with these guys. It's been a lot of fun. Playing in Coors Field, Denver, it's a great place."

And Tulowitzki agreed to a six-year, $31-million deal that will extend through what would have been his first year of free agency. The deal set a record in terms of money for a player with less than two full seasons of Major League experience, setting him up as the new face of the franchise into the next decade.

"Everybody knows the guys on this team are great baseball players," Tulowitzki said at the press conference announcing the deal. "But more than that, they're great guys. That's what makes it special.

"I took that into consideration and said, 'Wow, if we can really keep these core guys together, we have the makings to be something special. Now, the next step is keeping these guys together. I believe that is going to happen."

ACKNOWLEDGMENTS

To write a book of this sort, what you need, of course, are tales. And lots of them. To compile them, you need the time and cooperation of many, and the names that follow readily gave both. From a country club in Southern California, to restaurants in Tucson and Denver, to clubhouses in stadiums across the country—and of course at Coors Field—the many subjects I interviewed shared their stories and their remembrances. Owners, front-office types, managers, coaches, and players (including non-Rockies)—without them, this book wouldn't have been possible.

So here's a tip of the cap to: Jay Alves, Roger Bailey, Don Baylor, Buddy Bell, Dante Bichette, Craig Biggio, Vinny Castilla, Aaron Cook, Tony Cowell, Bobby Cox, Jerry Dipoto, Bob Gebhard, Todd Helton, Matt Holliday, Clint Hurdle, Jason Jennings, Chipper Jones, Kevin Kahn, Curtis Leskanic, Jim Leyland, Brent Mayne, Jerry McMorris, Charlie Monfort, Dan O'Dowd, Neifi Perez, Alan Roach, Tony Siegle, Jimmie Lee Solomon, Mark Strittmatter, Mike Swanson, Larry Walker, Walt Weiss, and Eric Young. Alves also gets credit for a couple of assists in helping to line up interviews. In truth, as long as that list is, it represents only a portion of 15 years of Rockies' history. There easily could be volumes II and III in this series, but this will have to do for now.

And now to my friends and colleagues in the media: Fans and

readers have no idea how much goes into the task of being a baseball beat writer. The Denver market has been fortunate to read some of the best: My former *Denver Post* Rockies beat-mates Jerry Crasnick, Jim Armstrong, Irv Moss, John Henderson, and Mike Klis; the *Post's* current heavy hitters Troy Renck, Patrick Saunders, Mark Kiszla, and Woody Paige; as well as Thomas Harding, Jack Etkin, and Tracy Ringolsby. Klis and Kiszla were particularly helpful in this effort.

Finally, thanks to the people at Sports Publishing, particularly John Humenik and editor Doug Hoepker. For a book is far more than a one-man show.

CLINT H URDLE—A MAN WITH A BIG HEART

When Clint Hurdle led his Colorado Rockies baseball team to a miraculous run to the National League pennant in 2007, he and his team became instant role models. But he always kept things in perspective, often saying, "Baseball's just a game." He learned five years earlier with the birth of his daughter, Madison, who was diagnosed with Prader-Willi syndrome (PWS), that real heroes are individuals who fight to live normal, healthy lives despite the obstacles presented by a serious health condition. As the national spokesperson for the Prader-Willi Syndrome Association (USA), Clint is to be commended for all he has done to improve the lives of those with PWS. He is the real hero in our book.

ABOUT PRADER-WILLI SYNDROME

PWS is a complex syndrome affecting appetite, growth, metabolism, cognitive function, and behavior. The hallmark characteristics of PWS are a constant hunger due to a dysfunction of the hypothalamus in the brain, and rapid weight gain on few calories because of a malfunctioning metabolic system. It is estimated that PWS affects one in 12,000 to 15,000 people, both sexes equally, and all ethnic groups. Currently there is no cure and no medications or procedures are successful in staving off the relentless hunger.

ABOUT PRADER-WILLI SYNDROME ASSOCIATION (USA)

PWSA (USA), a 501(c)(3) charity, is the only national membership organization that helps children and adults with PWS and their families through every stage of life. It was formed in 1975 to provide a vehicle of support for children with PWS, parents, and professionals. The organization funds PWS research and provides PWS support, education, and advocacy. Hospitals, physicians, and parents from all over the world consult with PWSA (USA) daily with medical emergencies and questions.

For more information about PWS or to make a donation in honor of Madison Hurdle, please contact PWSA (USA) toll-free at (800) 926-4797 or (941) 312-0400 or visit their Web site at www.pwsausa.org.

Prader-Willi Syndrome Association (USA)
8588 Potter Park Drive, Suite 500
Sarasota, FL 34238

Help us to help children like Madison Hurdle. They are hungry for a cure.